If You Want to Soar with Eagles,
Don't Hang out with Turkeys

If You Want to Soar with Eagles, Don't Hang out with Turkeys

Gems for Christian Living

Lois E. Scott

Illustrations by Caleb F. Scott
Edited by Fred W. Scott

If You Want to Soar with Eagles, Don't Hang out with Turkeys Gems for Christian Living

iUniverse books may be ordered through booksellers or by contacting:
iUniverse
1663 Liberty Drive
Bloomington, IN 47403
www.iuniverse.com
1-800-Authors (1-800-288-4677)

ISBN: 978-1-4401-2264-4 (sc)
ISBN: 978-1-4401-2265-1 (ebook)

Print information available on the last page.

iUniverse rev. date: 8/26/2015

This book is dedicated to our family, the Scott clan, pictured below at Caleb and Nicole Scott's wedding in 2008.

Contents

Foreword

My wife, Lois, has generated and collected pithy one-liners for the past thirty-five years. These one-liners can cut through the froth to the heart of a topic with wisdom, common sense, and often with humor. They may give comfort to a hurting person or challenge a teenager as he or she struggles to deal with this world. I call these one-liners *LOISisms*.

With these gems she has guided and instructed three sons and eleven grandchildren, and she is now working on seven great-grandchildren. Friends and family have enjoyed and have been challenged by her kitchen bar stool ministry. Lois would echo the words of John, the Elder: "I have no greater joy than to hear that my children are walking in the truth." (3 John 1:4) Lois and I are richly blessed with a large and loving family, and they all have a strong faith in Jesus Christ. This is due in no small part to the faith and ministry of Lois, or, as the Apostle Paul wrote to Timothy, "I have been reminded of your sincere faith, which first lived in your grandmother Lois, and in your mother Eunice and, I am persuaded, now lives in you also." (2 Timothy 1:5)

Lois has the gift of compassion. She has an uncanny ability to know when someone needs an encouraging word or a good laugh. She ministers to family, friends, and those who have fallen on hard times. For twenty-five years, she has volunteered once a week at Loaves & Fishes in Ithaca, helping to serve a free meal to 125–150 people who need a little help and a friendly smile or a hug. She is "Grandmother" to many of these needy people. Lois gave our collection of several years of *Our Daily Bread*, from which many of her gems came, to the library at the county jail so that the incarcerated also could be uplifted by these gems.

We hope these gems will give the reader a laugh or two. As the Christian comedian Ken Davis would say, "Lighten up and live!" If you are a believer in Jesus Christ, these gems may provide some food for thought as you live your life and raise your children. If you have not yet come to a saving relationship with the living Christ, Lois and I hope that some of these gems will challenge you to contemplate your relationship with Him, and hence your future beyond this limited time you have on this Earth.

Fred W. Scott
January 2010

Introduction

In 1951, at the age of seventeen, I started my search for God. I frequently babysat for our dear neighbors, who were distant relatives, farm folk, hard-working, and "salt of the earth" folks.

This dear couple had two baby boys, and both had cystic fibrosis. Dickie died at the age of two and a half on the night of my high school junior prom. I had been with him and his younger brother just the night before. I realized his suffering was over and felt in my heart that he was in more competent hands.

However, I asked myself over and over, "OK, God, why? If there is indeed a God—where are you?"

Dickie's brother lived for eighteen years, both in and out of hospitals. God was indeed merciful to these parents, for He gave them two more sons, strong and healthy boys.

My years from age sixteen (1950) to thirty-nine (1973) were exciting and happy years filled with high school, college, jobs, marriage, and family. Nothing earthshaking—normal, I would say, except for one problem. I truly had a God-shaped vacuum in my heart and knew something was lacking in my life.

My parents never went to the local church in town, but they let me go with the neighbors, my future husband Fred's mom and dad. We learned Bible stories in Sunday school, but I can't honestly recall any lessons about salvation. To me, being a Christian meant you weren't a Jew, so I was a Christian. As a family, though, we lived by the Golden Rule.

Coming from a dairy farm where we used Belgian draft horses to do the work, I learned at an early age to swear. I got the impression that swearing made them step lively, and swear I did until 1973, when this blaspheming just vanished.

My search intensified, and a certain group, popular in the Ithaca area, showed me a way of life that seemed exemplary. I felt compelled and drawn to listen and consider, but made no commitment. Thank God.

In 1973 the mother of a friend of our son Duane sensed this search in my life, and we went through the four spiritual laws together from a booklet printed by Campus Crusade for Christ International, entitled *How to Know God Personally*.

1. God loves you and offers a wonderful plan for your life.
2. All of us sin, and our sin has separated us from God.
3. Jesus Christ is God's only provision for our sin. Through Him we can know and experience God's love and plan for our life.
4. We must individually receive Jesus Christ as Savior and Lord; then we can know and experience God's love and plan for our lives.

Here comes the hang-up. I made no commitment on the spot because of my pride and the shock of discovering I wasn't a Christian. Instead I went home to ponder. Everyone has questions for God, and mine were the apple pie type—nothing new or different.

OK, God, what is it you want from me? My husband? One of my children? I opened my Bible down the middle, and guess what I saw? Psalm 127. This Psalm says: "Behold, children are a gift of the Lord." He spoke to me through this simple but powerful Scripture, and what He said was plain as day. "Well, bless your soul, Mrs. Scott, you know you can't make a blade of grass, so let's get on with it."

OK, God, You win. I prayed the prayer suggested in the Campus Crusade booklet: "Lord Jesus, I need You. Thank You for dying on the cross for my sins. I open the door of my life and receive You as my Savior and Lord. Thank You for forgiving my sins and giving me eternal life. Take control of the throne of my life. Make me the kind of person You want me to be."

No lightning or thunder occurred, but I knew I was different. Being normal, I wanted all my family members to be children of God— right now—or yesterday! However, I did not know how to share my newfound faith and freedom, and I discovered what it was like to be persecuted in my own home. That was a shock.

Also, being a New Englander, I found myself treating God like we used to treat new neighbors back in the Berkshire Hills of Massachusetts. We peeked from behind the curtains, so to speak, giving them a chance to prove themselves. If they passed the "curtain test," we accepted them. I've heard this kind of behavior referred to as *New England reserve.*

Six months later a situation arose, and I found myself in a bit of hot water. Without my newfound friend, Jesus, and my new but real faith in Him, the consequences could have been drastic. I called on Jesus Christ, the Son of the Living God, for the first time with true faith, and together we won. It comes as no shock to the Christian, but I must tell you anyway. He is real; He does live. The very name of Jesus, spoken among agnostics, is electrifying. The Holy Spirit, through me, was able to witness to these people, telling them of my newfound friend, Jesus. When I was told I was "different," it was truly exciting, and I was proud of the way my Jesus had stood and passed the "curtain test."

It seems the world system had confused me about the word *love.* We say *I love carrots, I love horses, I love to dance. I love my parents, my husband, my children.* Then there is *I will love you if …* you take the garbage out. Or *I love you because …* you ate your spinach. Love was very confusing to me.

The language of the people in New Testament times handled these different types of love more precisely, providing different names for different kinds of love. The love Jesus offers, the *I love you in spite of* kind of love, is *agape* love. Proof that we have really received this pure love from God is our new ability to love others *in spite of* whatever.

1 John 4:19 says, "We love, because He first loved us." We can forgive those whom we could never forgive and love those whom we dislike—not because we suddenly become good people, but because God has filled us to overflowing with His own love.

We become pipelines for divine love, and even a rusty pipeline can offer life-giving water. Through God's grace, I was able to share His love with my husband and three teenage sons, who all eventually came to accept Jesus Christ as their personal Savior.

With my newfound faith, I began collecting various sayings about faith and Christian living that I could share with family and friends.

This collection eventually resulted in writing this book in order to share these gems with a wider audience. Many of these one-liners came from *Our Daily Bread*, and from the writings, teaching, and humor of Pastor Chuck Swindoll. I am very appreciative to both for allowing their material to be included in *Eagles and Turkeys*. Enjoy!

Lois E. Scott
January 2010

Gems of Advice and Humor
for Christian Living

Animals

Any time you think you have influence, try ordering around someone else's dog. — *The Cockel Bur.*

Diplomacy is the art of saying "Nice doggie" until you can find a rock. — Will Rogers

Dogs have owners; cats have servants. — Unknown

Don't saddle a horse you can't ride. — Unknown

He who grabs a cat by the tail learns a lot about cats. — Mark Twain

Lois E. Scott

If you love something, set it free. If it comes back to you, it is yours. If it doesn't, it never was. — Richard Bach

If you pick up a starving dog and make him prosperous, he will not bite you. This is the principal difference between a dog and a man. — Mark Twain

If your dog thinks you're the greatest person in the world, don't seek a second opinion. — Jim Fiebig

If you want the best seat in the house, move the cat. — Unknown

It's not the size of the dog in the fight, it's the size of the fight in the dog. — Mark Twain

Live in such a way that you would not be ashamed to sell your parrot to the town gossip. — Will Rogers

One reason a dog is such a good friend is that his tail wags instead of his tongue. — Unknown

Rural Pearl's advice when a tool is borrowed: "Remember, it's not a cat. It won't come home by itself." — Donna Rhodes, *Country*, August/September 2006, p. 68.

The best doctor in the world is the veterinarian. He can't ask his patients what is the matter. He's got to just know. — Will Rogers

Bible

A Bible that's falling apart usually belongs to a person who isn't. — Frank A. Clark

A well-worn Bible is a sign of a well-fed soul. — *Our Daily Bread* (*ODB*), October 2004.

A world in darkness needs the light of the Gospel. — *ODB*, May 2003.

Bestsellers come and go, but the Word of God abides forever. — *ODB*, January 2006.

Deposit God's word in your memory bank, and you'll draw interest for life. — *ODB*, August 2002.

Gems of truth are found in the Bible—but you must dig for them. — *ODB*, January 2003.

God's Word is the compass that keeps us on course. — *ODB*, June 2006.

If you want life-changing mail, open your Bible and read a letter from God. — *ODB*, August 2003.

In all literature, there is nothing that compares with the Bible. — John Milton

Many books can inform you; only the Bible can transform you. — *ODB*, May 2003.

Many who have been blind to the truth have found that reading the Bible is a real eye-opener. — *ODB*, October 2003.

Most people are bothered by those passages of Scripture they do not understand, but the passages that bother me are those I do understand. — Mark Twain

One of the marks of a well-fed soul is a well-read Bible. — *ODB*, March 2003.

One truth from the Bible is worth more than all the wisdom of man. — *ODB*, April 2005.

People often say that motivation doesn't last. Well, neither does bathing. That's why we recommend it daily. — Zig Ziglar

Real truth, truth you can rely on, truth that will never turn sour, that will never backfire, that's the truth of the Bible. — Chuck Swindoll, *Growing Deep in the Christian Life*, p. 59.

Study the Bible to be wise; believe it to be safe; practice it to be holy. —*ODB*, February 2005.

The best commentary on the Bible is a person who puts it into practice. — *ODB*, January 2006.

The best TV guide is the Bible. — *ODB*, October 2003.

The best way to renew our minds is to read God's Word daily. — *ODB*, August 2005.

The better we know His Word, the more clearly we will know His will. — Chuck Swindoll, *Stress Fractures*, p. 241.

The Bible contains the vitamins for soul health. — *ODB*, August 2005.

The Bible isn't a dry book if you know the author. — *ODB*, June 2003.

The Bible will tell you what is wrong before you have done it! — Dwight L. Moody; *ODB*, September 2005.

The gospel is bad news to those who reject it and good news to those who receive it. — *ODB*, July 2005.

The profound truth that the Bible gives us is like a warm blanket wrapped around us on a cold night. — Chuck Swindoll, *Growing Deep in the Christian Life*, p. 66.

There is great security in opening God's timeless Book and hearing His voice. It calms our fears. It clears our heads. It comforts our hearts. Let it have its entrance today. — Chuck Swindoll, *The Quest for Character*, p. 186.

There is no more reliable authority on earth than God's Word, the Bible. — Chuck Swindoll, *Growing Deep in the Christian Life*, p. 55.

Think of the Bible as the absolutely reliable instrument panel designed to get people, and to keep people, on the right track. — Chuck Swindoll, *Stress Fractures*, p. 177.

We must adjust our lives to the Bible — never the Bible to our lives. — *ODB*, May 2003.

Your Word is a lamp to my feet and a light for my path. — Psalm 119:105.

Blessings

A thankful person enjoys a blessing twice—when it's received, and when it's remembered. — *ODB*, January 2002.

Adding up your blessings will multiply your joy. — *ODB*, October 2002.

Adversities are often blessings in disguise. — *ODB*, July 2005.

Blessed are the flexible, for we shall not be bent out of shape. — Bruce Dance

Blessed are the flexible, for they are pliable in God's hands. — J. David Hoke

Blessing is found along the pathway of duty. — *ODB*, March 2005.

Daily blessings are daily reminders of God. — *ODB*, June 2006.

Praise be to the Lord, to God our Savior, who daily bears our burdens. — Psalm 68:19.

Spend your time counting your blessings—not airing your complaints. — *ODB*, April 2002, March 2005.

To conquer the habit of complaining, count your blessings. — *ODB*, September 2003.

Lois E. Scott

To live in the past is to miss today's opportunities and tomorrow's blessings. — *ODB*, February 2002.

We add to our problems when we fail to count our blessings. — *ODB*, February 2002.

We cry out easily when we have only a little pain. We smile but little for our many blessings. — Unknown

With unwanted burdens come undeserved blessings. — *ODB*, January 2005.

Children

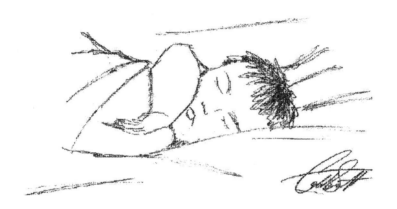

A baby is a heart with arms and legs. — Unknown

Any child can tell you that the sole purpose of a middle name is so he can tell when he's really in trouble. — Dennis Fakes

Ask your child what he wants for dinner only if he's buying. — Fran Lebowitz

Big lessons can be learned from little children. — *ODB*, March 2004, June 2002.

Children are likely to live up to what you believe of them. — Lady Bird Johnson

Children are not things to be molded, but people to be unfolded. — Jess Lair

Children begin by loving their parents; as they grow older, they judge them; sometimes they forgive them. — Oscar Wilde

Feel the dignity of a child. Do not feel superior to him, for you are not. — Robert Henri

For excellence, ask an expert; for wisdom, ask a sage; for honesty, ask a child. — J. Van Dyke, *Words to Live By.*

God's children never say good-bye for the last time. — *ODB*, September 2004.

Grandchildren are God's way of compensating us for growing old. — Mary H. Waldrip

Grown-ups never understand anything for themselves, and it is tiresome for children to be always and forever explaining things to them. — Antoine de Saint-Exupéry

Human beings are the only creatures that allow their children to come back home. — Bill Cosby

I have no greater joy than to hear that my children are walking in the truth. — 3 John 1:4.

I was not a child prodigy, because a child prodigy is a child who knows as much when it is a child as it does when it grows up. — Will Rogers

If you want boys to do a job, remember that one boy is a boy; two boys are half a boy; and three boys are no boys at all. — Eugene Alt, *Country*, August/September 2006.

Little children are of great value to God. — *ODB*, May 2006.

Never have children, only grandchildren. — Gore Vidal

No man stands so tall as when he stoops to help a child. — Abraham Lincoln

People who say they sleep like a baby usually don't have one. — Leo J. Burke

Sleep on, my child. The world is waiting for you. — From a lullaby.

Small enough to hold in your arms and big enough to fill your world. There's nothing in the whole wide world as lovable as a baby boy. — Unknown

The best way to keep children home is to make the home atmosphere pleasant — and let the air out of the tires. — Dorothy Parker

The difference between a high-spirited child and a juvenile delinquent is whether he is my kid or yours. — Jo Petty, *Bits of Silver and Gold, Love.*

There was never a child so lovely but his mother was glad to get him asleep. — Ralph Waldo Emerson

When talking with a small child, get down on your knees; otherwise, all he will remember is the hair in your nose.

You know that children are growing up when they start asking questions that have answers. — John J. Plomp

Christian Living

A cheerful look brings joy to the heart, and good news gives health to the bones. — Proverbs 15:30.

A Christian's life is a window through which others can see Jesus. — *ODB*, June 2006.

A cloudy day is no match for a sunny disposition. — William Arthur Ward

A disciple of Jesus Christ leaves everything better than he found it. — Unknown

A divided heart multiplies our problems. — *ODB*, August 2003.

A faith that costs nothing and demands nothing is worth nothing. — *ODB*, October 2004.

A fruitful harvest requires faithful service. — *ODB*, September 2003.

After a storm, the birds sing—why shouldn't [we]? — Rose F. Kennedy

A good motive turns bad on the hinge of selfishness. — *ODB*, September 2004.

A good test of character: When you do wrong, do you accept the blame? — *ODB*, January 2003.

A grudge is one thing that does not get better when it is nursed. — *ODB*, May 2004.

A heartfelt apology can't change the past, but it can brighten the future. — *ODB*, August 2005.

A kind word is the oil that takes the friction out of life. — *ODB*, October 2004.

A lie is a coward's attempt to get out of trouble. — *ODB*, January 2004.

A life lived for God leaves a lasting legacy. — *ODB*, October 2004.

A little light makes a big difference in the darkest night. — *ODB*, October 2003.

A man of words and not of deeds is like a garden full of weeds. — Percy B. Green, *A History of Nursery Rhymes*, 1899.

A man's heart plans his way, but the Lord directs his steps. — Proverbs 16:9.

A merry heart does good, like a medicine, but a broken spirit dries the bones. — Proverbs 17:22.

Anger is just one letter short of danger. — *ODB*, January 2006.

An interruption may be a divine appointment. — *ODB*, March 2006.

A person may go wrong in many different directions but right in only one. — *ODB*, October 2004.

A person reveals his character by nothing so clearly as the joke he resents. — Georg Christoph Lichtenberg

A sense of humor is part of the art of leadership, of getting along with people, of getting things done. — Dwight D. Eisenhower

A single light can provide hope in the darkest night. — *ODB*, April 2005.

A song in the heart puts a smile on the face. — *ODB*, January 2004.

A spark of encouragement can rekindle warmth in the heart. — *ODB*, March 2003.

A tunnel of testing can produce a shining testimony. — *ODB*, January 2003.

A word of encouragement can make the difference between giving up or going on. — *ODB*, July 2003.

Above all else, guard your heart, for it is the wellspring of life. — Proverbs 4:23.

Actions speak louder than bumper stickers. — *ODB*, July 2004.

All wise men share one trait—the ability to listen. — Frank Tyger

Although the outlook may be bleak, the uplook is always bright. — *ODB*, June 2003.

An attitude of gratitude can make your life a beatitude. — *ODB*, November 2000.

As the Shepherd goes, so go the sheep. — Unknown

Avoid guilt and shame: Guilt is the psychic pain, and shame is loss of face or embarrassment. — Unknown

Be the best at whatever you do. If you dig ditches, dig the best ditches ever. — Unknown

Beware—the more you look at temptation, the better it looks. — *ODB*, October 2003.

Beware the barrenness of a busy day. — Redpath; *ODB*, January 2002.

Be with people who make you want to be a better person. It is important that the people around you encourage your virtues and not your vices. — Unknown

Build bridges of trust that will bear the weight of truth. — Ron Bennett

Change is the law of life. And those who look only to the past or the present are certain to miss the future. — John F. Kennedy

Character cannot be developed in ease and quiet. Only through experience of trial and suffering can the soul be strengthened, ambition inspired, and success achieved. — Helen Keller

Character, in the long run, is the decisive factor in the life of an individual and of nations alike. — Theodore Roosevelt

Character is formed by making choices in one direction. — *ODB*, February 2005.

Christianity is the life of God in the soul of man. — Henry Scougal

Christians are like coals of fire—together, they glow; apart, they grow cold. — *ODB*, July 2004.

Christians must live in the world, but not let the world live in them. — *ODB*, January 2002.

Christians never say good-bye to each other for the last time. — *ODB*, November 2003.

Christians worth their salt make others thirsty for the water of life. — *ODB*, July 2005.

Clothe yourselves with the Lord Jesus Christ. — Romans 13:14.

Commit to the Lord whatever you do, and your plans will succeed. — Proverbs 16:3.

Constantly choosing the lesser of two evils is still choosing evil. — Jerry Garcia

Correction does much, but encouragement does more. — *ODB*, October 2003.

Criticism is a good teacher if we are willing to learn from it. — *ODB*, January 2003.

Decay starts when growth stops. — *ODB*, September 2004.

Discipline is the disciple's "career." — Unknown

Do not make friends with a hot-tempered man, do not associate with one easily angered, or you may learn his ways and get yourself ensnared. — Proverbs 22:24–25.

Doing an injury puts you below your enemy. Revenging one makes you but even with him. Forgiving one sets you above him. — Benjamin Franklin

Doing what you said you would do is simply an issue of integrity. There is no substitute for having the guts to keep your word. — Chuck Swindoll, *Rise and Shine*, p. 191.

Don't be so busy doing good that you neglect to do what's right. — *ODB*, September 2006.

Don't just count your days, make your days count. — *ODB*, January 2004.

Don't just get older, get better. Live realistically. Give generously. Adapt willingly. Trust fearlessly. Rejoice daily. — Chuck Swindoll, *Strike the Original Match*, p. 182.

Every time we encourage someone, we give them a transfusion of courage. — Chuck Swindoll, *Growing Deep in the Christian Life*, p. 380.

Every word we say on earth is heard in heaven. — *ODB*, July 2003.

Everyone is valuable to God. — *ODB*, January 2003.

Faith in Christ enables us to live above our circumstances, not under them! — *ODB*, April 2002.

Families are like quilts; lives pieced together, stitched with smiles and tears, colored with memories, and bound by love. — Copyrighted poem, used with permission of Renee Baker, author.

Feeding your faith will starve your doubts. — *ODB*, March 2003.

Feeling let down today? Try looking up. — *ODB*, December 2004.

Filter everything through the same question: Will this bring glory to God or to me? — Chuck Swindoll, *Rise and Shine*, p. 33.

> Find out what God would have you do
> and do that little well.
> For what is great and what is small
> the Lord alone can tell.
> — Unknown

Followers of Christ should focus on what unites them, not on what divides them. — *ODB*, November 2005.

Following Jesus is not always easy, but it's always right. — *ODB*, January 2005.

Following Jesus takes the busyness out of life. — *ODB*, July 2005.

For when the One Great Scorer comes to write against your name, He'll write not that you won or lost, but how you played the game. — Grantland Rice

Forgiving one's enemies does not mean to be fainthearted, but to have a strong soul. — Italian Proverb

Give the world the best you have and you'll get kicked in the teeth. Give the world the best you have anyway. — Mother Teresa

Give your life to God; He can do more with it than you can! — Dwight L. Moody

God gives strength in proportion to the strain. — *ODB*, February 2003.

God gives us all we need, so we can give to those in need. — *ODB*, July 2003.

God has not promised to keep us from life's storms, but to keep us through them. — *ODB*, June 2003.

God has promised forgiveness to your repentance, but He has not promised tomorrow to your procrastination. — St. Augustine of Hippo

God helps those who know they are helpless. — *ODB*, June 2003.

God never fails to give credit where credit is due. — *ODB*, March 2003.

God stretches our patience to enlarge our soul. — *ODB*, March 2003.

God's easy yoke does not fit on a stiff neck. — *ODB*, January 2005.

God's generous giving deserves thankful living. — *ODB*, March 2003.

God's justice leaves no room for prejudice. — *ODB*, January 2003.

God's reputation is at stake in my life. I want to maintain it, not stain it. — Bruce Wilkerson, *Your Daily Walk*, 1991, p. 55.

God's strength is best seen in our weakness. — *ODB*, June 2003.

Godliness is true greatness. — *ODB*, February 2002.

Good, better, best. Never let it rest … until good is better and better is best. — Adlai Stevenson

Good deeds are no substitute for the Good News. — *ODB*, January 2002.

Good intentions are no good until they are put into action. — *ODB*, January 2005.

Good intentions are no substitute for obedience. — *ODB*, January 2003.

Gratitude should be a continuous attitude. — *ODB*, September 2005.

Happiness depends on what you are, not on what you have. — *ODB*, December 2003.

Happiness, like winning, is a matter of right thinking, not intelligence, age, or position. — Chuck Swindoll, *Come before Winter*, p. 239.

Hard work spotlights the character of people: some turn up their sleeves, some turn up their noses, and some don't turn up at all. — Sam Ewing

He must become greater; I must become less. — John 3:30.

He who laughs, lasts. — *ODB*, July 2004.

Hearts in tune with God will sing His praises. — *ODB*, July 2003.

Hold loosely to what is temporal and tightly to what is eternal. — *ODB*, December 2000.

Honesty and frankness make you vulnerable. Be honest anyway. — Mother Teresa

Honesty is the best policy. — Benjamin Franklin

Honesty means never having to look over your shoulder. — *ODB*, February 2003.

Humbition—having ambition enough to keep reaching toward your full capacity as a human being, and humility enough to admit your natural limitations. — Jane Harper

Humility is a paradox; the moment you think you've finally found it, you've lost it. And yet, God expects (and rewards) an attitude of servant-like humility in His followers. — Unknown

Hymns for speeding:

- at 45 mph = "God will take care of you"
- at 55 mph = "Guide me, O thou Great Jehovah"
- at 65 mph = "Nearer, my God, to thee"
- at 75 mph = "Nearer, still nearer"
- at 85 mph = "This world is not my home"
- at 95 mph = "Lord, I'm coming home"
- over 100 mph = "Precious memories"
— Pastor Tim, <http://www.talkjesus.com/jokes/14117-speeding-hymns.html>

I do not think much of a man who is not wiser today than he was yesterday. — Abraham Lincoln, *Country*, August/September 2006, p. 5.

I long to accomplish great and noble tasks, but it is my chief duty to accomplish humble tasks as though they were great and noble. — Helen Keller, quoted by David Jeremiah

I'm afraid that some long-faced saints would crack their concrete masks if they smiled—I really am! Nothing repels like a frown—or attracts like a smile. — Chuck Swindoll, *Encourage Me*, p. 70.

I'm just a nobody telling everybody about Somebody who can save anybody! — *ODB*, April 2004.

If it is to be, it is up to me. (ten two-letter words) — Unknown

If we have hope, we can go on. — *ODB*, September 2005.

If you are too big to do the small jobs, you are too small to do the big jobs. — Unknown

If you are not as close to God as you once were, make no mistake about who moved. — Unknown

If you are successful, you win false friends and true enemies. Succeed anyway. — Mother Teresa

If you can't sleep, don't count sheep—talk to the Shepherd. — Church sign

If you do good, people will accuse you of selfish and ulterior motives. Do good anyway. — Mother Teresa

If you don't live it, you don't believe it. — Unknown

If you think you know everything, you have a lot to learn. — *ODB*, January 2003.

If you want to leave footprints in the sands of time, wear work shoes. — *ODB*, April 2006.

If your Christian life is a drag, worldly weights may be holding you back. — *ODB*, March 2005.

In any moment of decision, the best thing you can do is the right thing. The worst thing you can do is nothing. — Theodore Roosevelt, *Country*, August/September 2006, p. 4.

In acceptance we find peace. — *ODB*, May 2003.

In every lonely place, God surrounds us with angels. — Unknown

In everything, do to others what you would have them do to you. Matthew 7:12.

In tough times, God teaches us to trust. — *ODB*, January 2003.

Instead of complaining about the thorns on roses, be thankful for the roses among the thorns. —*ODB*, August 2003, May 2004.

Instead of using the word *problem*, try substituting the word *opportunity*. — H. Jackson Brown, Jr.

It is easier to resist the first evil desire than to satisfy all the ones that follow. — *ODB*, September 2004.

It is in pardoning that we are pardoned. — Jo Petty, *Bits of Silver and Gold, Love.*

It is not the end of joy that makes old age so sad, but the end of hope. — Jean Paul Richter

It is right that we remember wrongs done to us so that we may forgive them. — Jo Petty, *Bits of Silver and Gold, Love.*

It's always darkest before the dawn. — *ODB*, March 2005.

It's always too soon to quit. — *ODB*, April 2003.

It's better to give others a piece of your heart than a piece of your mind. — *ODB*, August 2004.

It's not enough to know God with your head; you must know Him in your heart. — *ODB*, July 2005.

It's the life behind the words that makes your testimony effective. — *ODB*, November 2004.

Joseph had it right! Trust God. Wait patiently. Watch expectantly. — David Jeremiah

Keep your thoughts in line, or they'll lead you astray. — *ODB*, March 2005.

Kind words can give a lift to a heavy heart. — *ODB*, October 2003.

Kindness is always in season. — *ODB*, December 2003.

Kindness is the oil that takes the friction out of life. — *ODB*, November 2005.

Leaders don't attain greatness by giving orders, but by serving others. — *ODB*, August 2003.

Let God's promises shine on your problems. — Corrie ten Boom

Let your light so shine before men, that they may see your good works, and glorify your Father which is in heaven. — Matthew 5:16

Live today as if you will stand before God tomorrow. — *ODB*, February 2005.

Living for the Lord leaves a lasting legacy. — *ODB*, January 2003.

Living only for temporary gain leads to eternal loss. — *ODB*, August 2003.

Look for things to laugh at—and laugh out loud. It's biblical. — Chuck Swindoll, *Stress Fractures*, p. 168.

Losing your temper is no way to get rid of it. — *ODB*, October 2000.

Make the very most of all you've got, and make the very least of what you can't get yet. — Unknown

Many people readily give God credit, but few cheerfully give Him cash. — *ODB*, October 2004.

Memories are a gift from God that death cannot destroy. — Unknown

Men show their character in nothing more clearly than in what they think laughable. — Johann Wolfgang von Goethe

Mind what you say, or you might say whatever comes to mind. — *ODB*, January 2005.

Miracle—a coincidence where God chooses to remain anonymous. — Unknown

More attention should be given to making a life than making a living. — Unknown

Neither vice nor virtue can remain a secret forever. — *ODB*, September 2004.

No man is poor who has had a godly mother. — Abraham Lincoln

No one is old who is young at heart. — *ODB*, August 2004.

No one would remember the Good Samaritan if he had only had good intentions. — Margaret Thatcher

Nobodies … exalting Somebody. Are you one? Listen to me! It's the "nobodies" Somebody chooses so carefully. And when He has selected you for that role, He does not consider you a nobody. — Chuck Swindoll, *Growing Strong in the Seasons*, p. 129.

Nobody wins when we play favorites. — *ODB*, October 2003.

Nothing can dim the beauty that shines from within. — *ODB*, November 2005.

Obedience is faith in action. — *ODB*, February 2002.

Often it's the joy behind our words that makes our testimony ring true. — *ODB*, March 2003.

Oh, well, He never promised me a rose garden. — Jane Mall

Once a man feels he is in the center of God's will, he is invincible. — Unknown

One little word can spare a lot of trouble. It's no. — *ODB*, September 2004.

Only the one who has learned to serve is qualified to lead. — *ODB*, March 2003.

Only when we are changed can we help others to change. — *ODB*, March 2003.

Opportunity alone does not constitute the will of God. — Unknown

Our character is only as strong as our behavior. — *ODB*, March 2005.

Our day's work isn't done until we build up someone. — *ODB*, March 2003.

Our rough edges must be chipped away to bring out the image of Christ. — *ODB*, February 2002.

Peace I leave with you; my peace I give you. I do not give to you as the world gives. Do not let your hearts be troubled and do not be afraid. — John 14:27.

Peace is the ability to wait patiently in spite of panic brought on by uncertainty. — Chuck Swindoll, *Stress Fractures*, p. 50.

People are unreasonable, illogical, and self-centered. Love them anyway. — Mother Teresa

People really need help, but may attack you if you help them. Help them anyway. — Mother Teresa

People who follow Christ lead others in the right direction. — *ODB*, May 2002.

Personality can open doors, but only character can keep them open. — Elmer G. Letterman

Praise loudly, blame softly. — *ODB*, February 2005.

Resentment comes from looking at others; contentment comes from looking to God. — *ODB*, November 2003.

Respect individuality. — Unknown

Revenge gets you even with your enemy; forgiveness puts you above him. — *ODB*, May 2003.

Right thinking leads to right living. — *ODB*, March 2003, September 2004.

Self-pity is the smog that pollutes and obscures the light of the Son. — Chuck Swindoll, *Growing Strong in the Seasons of Life*, p. 337.

Show me how a man treats his animals and I will show you what he thinks of people. — Unknown

Small minds discuss people, average minds discuss happenings, great minds discuss ideas. — Unknown

Sometimes God has to take away what we have so He can give us what He really wants us to have. He doesn't make mistakes. — Unknown

Tell me what a man believes and I'll tell you what he'll do. — Unknown

The best way to get even is to forgive. — *ODB*, November 2000.

The better we know ourselves, the less we'll criticize others. — *ODB*, February 2002.

The character of a man is known from his conversation. — Menander

The cost of obedience is nothing compared with the cost of disobedience. — *ODB*, March 2003.

The flowers or weeds that spring up tomorrow are in the seeds we sow today. — *ODB*, May 2003.

The future is bright if Christ is your hope. — *ODB*, June 2003.

The glory of God is man fully alive.. — St. Irenaeus of Lyons

The God who delivered us yesterday is worthy of our obedience today. — *ODB*, February 2003.

The good you do will be forgotten tomorrow. Do good anyway. — Mother Teresa

The great use of life is to spend it for something that will outlast it. — William James

The hardest thing to learn in life is which bridge to cross and which one to burn. — David Russell

The Holy Spirit is the Christian's power supply. — *ODB*, May 2002.

The human spirit soars with hope when lifted by an encouraging word. — *ODB*, March 2005.

The joy of the Lord is your strength. — Nehemiah 8:10.

The meaning of life cannot be told; it has to happen to a person. — Unknown

The more Son you get, the less likely you'll burn. — Nancy E. Stahlman

The most deceptive liars are those who live on the edge of truth. — *ODB*, July 2003.

The next person you meet may be your mission field. — *ODB*, October 2004.

The only leaders qualified to lead are those who have learned to serve. — *ODB*, February 2004.

The optimist says the cup is half full. The pessimist says the cup is half empty. The child of God says, "My cup runneth over." — Unknown

The seeds of wrongdoing may be sown in secret, but the crop cannot be concealed. — *ODB*, October 2004.

The things that count most in life are the things that cannot be counted. — Bernard Meltzer

The two most important requirements for major success are: first, being in the right place at the right time; and second, doing something about it. — Ray Kroc

The very best platform upon which we may build a case for Christianity at work rests on six massive pillars: integrity, faithfulness, punctuality, quality workmanship, a pleasant attitude, and enthusiasm. — Chuck Swindoll, *Growing Strong in the Seasons of Life*, p. 86.

The world is watching us—do they see Jesus? — *ODB*, November 2004.

The world sees what we do—God sees why we do it. — *ODB*, July 2004.

There's no better sermon than a good example. — *ODB*, July 2005.

They will be called oaks of righteousness, a planting of the Lord for the display of His splendor. — Isaiah 61:3.

Things turn out the best for those who make the best of the way things turn out. — John Wooden

This day and your life, my friend, are God's gifts to you—so give thanks and be joyful always. — Jim Beggs

Those who know God will be humble; those who know themselves cannot be proud. — *ODB*, January 2003.

To ease another's burden, help to carry it. — *ODB*, April 2003, July 2006.

To find your way through life, follow Jesus. — *ODB*, March 2003.

To get out of a hard situation, try a soft answer. — *ODB*, July 2003.

To get the most out of life, make every moment count for Christ. — *ODB*, November 2003.

To have a fulfilling life, let God fill you. — *ODB*, July 2003.

To lead others out of the darkness, let them see your light. — *ODB*, December 2003.

To live for Christ, we must die to self. — *ODB*, March 2003.

To put failure behind you, face up to it. — *ODB*, August 2004.

To refuse praise is to seek praise twice. — Unknown

To resent and remember brings strife; to forgive and forget brings peace. — *ODB*, January 2002.

To reveal error, expose it to the light of God's truth. — *ODB*, January 2003.

To silence gossip, don't repeat it. — *ODB*, January 2003, February 2003.

To stay youthful, stay useful. — *ODB*, March 2006.

To stretch the truth is to tell a lie. — *ODB*, April 2003.

To survive the storms of life, be anchored to the Rock of Ages. — *ODB*, January 2004.

Today—that special block of time holding the key that locks out yesterday's nightmares and unlocks tomorrow's dreams. — Chuck Swindoll, *The Quest for Character*, p. 15.

True integrity implies you do what is right when no one is looking or when everyone is compromising. — Chuck Swindoll, *Rise and Shine*, p. 198.

True submission is humility acquired on behalf of another. — Unknown

Trust God to move your mountain, but keep on climbing. — *ODB*, March 2005.

Truth is not determined by how many people believe it. — *ODB*, January 2003.

Wanted: Messengers to deliver the Good News. — *ODB*, January 2002.

We are all faced with a series of great opportunities—brilliantly disguised as insoluble problems. — John W. Gardner; Lee Iacocca; Chuck Swindoll

We are all missionaries. Wherever we go, we either bring people nearer to Christ, or we repel them from Christ. — Eric Liddell

We are shaped and fashioned by what we love. — Johann Wolfgang von Goethe

We can accomplish more together than we can alone. — *ODB*, February 2003.

We can learn more from sorrow than from laughter. — *ODB*, May 2003.

We cannot choose most circumstances that life may deliver to us; however, we can always choose how we will respond in our adversities. — Duane D. Scott

We don't need more to be thankful for, we just need to be more thankful. — *ODB*, May 2003.

We fall into temptation when we don't flee from it. — *ODB*, January 2005.

We honor God our Father when we live like His Son. — *ODB*, February 2003.

We inherit more from our parents than we are willing to admit. — Unknown

We must learn to weep before we can dry another's tears. — *ODB*, October 2003.

We need a world view of what God is doing—be world changers. — Unknown

We witness best for Christ when we say the least about ourselves. — *ODB*, January 2003.

What you spent years building may be destroyed overnight. Build anyway. — Mother Teresa

What you will be tomorrow depends on the choices you make today. — *ODB*, November 2005.

When the character of a man is not clear to you, look at his friends. — Japanese Proverb

When the going gets too easy, you may be going downhill — *ODB*, November 2000.

When we walk with the Lord, we'll be out of step with the world. — *ODB*, January 2005.

When you stop changing, you stop growing. — *ODB*, November 2000.

When you taste God's goodness, His praise will be on your lips. — *ODB*, June 2003.

Whenever we fall, it is usually at the point where we think we are strong. — *ODB*, July 2005.

Where there is no "moral gravity," no force that draws us to the center, there is a spiritual weightlessness. — Unknown

With God on our side we are never outnumbered. — *ODB*, May 2003.

Without mercy all of us are without hope. — Jo Petty, *Bits of Silver and Gold, Love*.

Words can't break bones, but they can break hearts. — *ODB*, December 22, 2004.

You and I become what we think about. — Chuck Swindoll, *Come Before Winter*, p. 238.

You are responsible to do the best you can with what you've got for as long as you're able. — Chuck Swindoll, *Come Before Winter*, p. 99.

You can have fun and still be efficient. In fact, you will be more efficient! — Chuck Swindoll, *Stress Fractures*, p. 155.

Lois E. Scott

You can tell the character of every man when you see how he receives praise. — Lucius Annaeus Seneca

You can tell a lot about a fellow's character by his way of eating jelly beans. — Ronald Reagan

You can't glorify yourself and Christ at the same time. — *ODB*, October 2004.

You can't lose when you help others win. — *ODB*, May 2004.

You can't speak a kind word too soon, for you never know how soon it will be too late. — *ODB*, July 2003.

You cannot hide your influence. — *ODB*, April 2005.

34

You don't need to know where you're going if you're following the Shepherd. — *ODB*, October 2003.

You have to prove that you mean what you say or else stop saying it. — Unknown

You won't fall for what's wrong if you stand for what's right. — *ODB*, July 2003.

You won't get indigestion by swallowing your pride. — *ODB*, February 2004.

Your day usually goes the way the corners of your mouth are turned. — Unknown

Lois E. Scott

Your decision about Jesus determines your destiny. — *ODB*, March 2005.

Your life either sheds light or casts a shadow. — *ODB*, January 2006.

Your response to temptation will make you or break you. — *ODB*, March 2005.

Your walk talks and your talk walks, but your walk talks louder than your talk walks. — Unknown

Church

A church can become a graveyard if its members bury their gifts. — *ODB*, September 2001.

A church helps the lost to find their way home when its light shines brightly. — *ODB*, November 2003.

A church is not a museum for saints, but a hospital for sinners. — Abigail Van Buren

A church's health is measured by its sending capacity, not its seating capacity. — Rick Warren, *The Purpose Driven Church*, p. 32.

A Great Commitment to the Great Commandment and the Great Commission will grow a Great Church! — Rick Warren, *The Purpose Driven Church*, p. 102.

A pastor leads best when his people get behind him. — *ODB*, July 2003.

A world in despair needs churches that care. — *ODB*, September 2005.

Changed lives are a church's greatest advertisement. — Rick Warren, *The Purpose Driven Church*, p. 222.

Don't wait for six strong men to take you to church. — Church sign

God's not on vacation—join us! — Church sign

Grow the church from the outside in, rather than from the inside out. — Rick Warren, *The Purpose Driven Church*, p. 138.

Growing churches focus on reaching receptive people. Nongrowing churches focus on reenlisting inactive people. — Rick Warren, *The Purpose Driven Church*, p. 183.

Hymns for Seasoned Citizens:

- The Old Rugged Face
- Precious Lord, Take My Hand, and Help Me Up
- It Is Well with My Soul, but My Knees Hurt
- Nobody Knows the Trouble I Have Seeing
- Amazing Grace, Considering My Age
- Just a Slower Walk with Thee
- Count Your Many Birthdays, Name Them One by One
- Go Tell It on the Mountain, but Speak Up
- Give Me That Old Timers' Religion
- Blessed Insurance
- Guide Me, O Thou Great Jehovah, I've Forgotten Where I Parked

— Paul Heil, TGG Newsletter, August 28, 2007.

Increasing the size of your church is simple: You must get more people to visit! — Rick Warren, *The Purpose Driven Church*, p. 252.

Long before the pastor preaches, the visitors are already deciding if they will come back. — Rick Warren, *The Purpose Driven Church*, p. 211.

Never confuse methods with the message. The message must never change, but the methods must change with each new generation. — Rick Warren, *The Purpose Driven Church*, p. 61.

Our world is filled with lonely people who are starving for the affirmation of a loving touch. — Rick Warren, *The Purpose Driven Church*, p. 214.

Seven days without church makes one weak. — *ODB*, July 2003.

Sitting in a church no more makes one a Christian than sitting in a garage makes one a car. — Hal Lindsey

The church is a training center, not a country club. — *ODB*, June 2001.

The church, rooted in God, can never be uprooted by man. — *ODB*, October 2003.

The depth of a church is determined by its quality of worship and instruction. The breadth of a church is determined by its commitment to fellowship and evangelism. — Chuck Swindoll, *Rise and Shine*, p. 70.

The warm fellowship of the church will keep your heart from growing old. — *ODB*, September 2003.

There are two kinds of people who go to church these days. There are the pillars of the church who stand underneath the load and carry the weight. And there are the caterpillars of the church who crawl in and out each Sunday and never do anything. — Howard Hendricks, Dallas Theological Seminary, quoted by David Jeremiah, *Turning Points*, June 2006, p. 18.

There is no insignificant task in the church. — *ODB*, July 2005.

There will be times a church must be steel, and other times it will have to be velvet. A church that is all steel is harsh and calculating. A church that is all velvet becomes too soft, too tolerant, accepting anything and lacking in conviction. — Chuck Swindoll, *Rise and Shine*, p. 91.

Think of church like a huddle at a football game: You and I know that teams don't show up simply to huddle. They huddle only long enough to know the plays. Through the week we run the plays. Sunday after Sunday we return to the huddle and get the plays. — Chuck Swindoll, *Rise and Shine*, p. 69.

We have an I-centered generation of church attenders who have decided that the church is a place for getting instead of giving. — David Jeremiah, *Turning Points*, June 2006, p. 17.

We never did it that way before. — Ralph W. Neighbour, *The Seven Last Words of the Church*, Zondervan Pub. House, Grand Rapids, MI (1973).

Weak excuses keep some people from church week after week. — *ODB*, July 2003.

Committees

A committee can make a decision that is dumber than any of its members. — David Coblitz

A committee is a cul-de-sac down which ideas are lured and then quietly strangled. — Sir Barnett Cocks

A moose is a horse created by a committee. — Unknown

Committee—a group of men who individually can do nothing but as a group decide that nothing can be done. — Fred Allen

Deacon's explanation of the confusing layout of his church: "It was designed by a committee." — Fred Scott

Forget committees. New, noble, world-changing ideas always come from one person working alone. — H. Jackson Brown, Jr.

If a thing is urgent, do it yourself. If not, form a committee. — Unknown

Meetings are indispensable when you don't want to do anything. — John Kenneth Galbraith

The only thing that comes out of a committee meeting is a lukewarm solution to a red-hot problem. — Robert M. Miller, *The Best of RMM*, 1:55.

There is no monument dedicated to the memory of a committee. — Lester J. Pourciau

To get something done, a committee should consist of no more than three men, two of whom are absent. — Robert Copeland

Evangelism

Do we have a burden for the lost, or have we lost our burden? — *ODB*, May 2002.

Evangelism is nothing more than one beggar telling another beggar where to find bread. — *ODB*, July 2002.

No one can bypass Jesus and get to heaven. — *ODB*, June 2003.

Open your ears to God before you open your mouth to others. — *ODB*, June 2003.

Rise and shine, friend. Everyone you meet today is on heaven's Most Wanted List. — Chuck Swindoll, *Rise and Shine*, p. 71.

Faith

A living faith is a working faith. — *ODB*, February 2003.

Faith in Christ is not just a single step—it's a lifelong walk with Him. — *ODB*, September 2005.

Faith is the strength by which a shattered world shall emerge into the light. — Helen Keller

Faith sees what the eyes cannot. — *ODB*, April 2002.

God still desires to impact our generation with remarkable families of faith—that includes you and your family. — Chuck Swindoll, *Growing Wise in Family Life*, p. 25.

Praise is the voice of faith. — *ODB*, May 2003.

Sorrow looks back. Worry looks around. Faith looks up. — Unknown

Thank the Lord for the faith that frees the love that knows it cannot lose its own. — Jo Petty, *Bits of Silver and Gold, Love*.

Friendship

A faithful friend is a true image of the Deity. — Napoleon Bonaparte

A friend is a person with whom I may be sincere. Before him, I may think aloud. — Ralph Waldo Emerson

A friend is someone who knows all about you and still loves you. — Elbert Hubbard

A friend to all is a friend to none. — Aristotle

A man's friendships are one of the best measures of his worth. — Charles Darwin

A path to a friend's house is never long. — Danish Proverb

A real friend is one who walks in when the rest of the world walks out. — Walter Winchell

A true friend is like support to a leaning wall. — *ODB*, August 2006.

A true friend stays true to the end. — *ODB*, June 2005.

Be slow in choosing a friend, slower in changing. — Benjamin Franklin

Before you put on a frown, my friend, make absolutely certain there are no smiles available. — Jim Beggs

Choose thy friends like thy books, few but choice. — James Howell

Empathy = your pain in my heart. — *ODB*, September 2005.

Friends are like melons; shall I tell you why? To find one good you must a hundred try. — Claude Mermet

If you ever see a man without a smile, give him one of yours. — Proverb

Laughter is not a bad beginning for a friendship, and it is the best ending for one. — Oscar Wilde

Our job is not to see through one another, but to see one another through. — Unknown

"Stay" is a charming word in a friend's vocabulary. — Amos Bronson Alcott

The holy passion of Friendship is of so sweet and steady and loyal and enduring a nature that it will last through a whole lifetime, if not asked to lend money. — Mark Twain

The only rose without thorns is friendship. — Madeleine de Scudéry

The only safe and sure way to destroy your enemy is to make him your friend. — Abraham Lincoln

The time to make friends is before you need them. — Ethel Barrymore

There are no strangers in the world, only friends waiting to be met. — Unknown

To find fulfillment, my friend, don't coexist with life—embrace it! — Jim Beggs

Treasure is not always a friend, but a friend is always a treasure. — Unknown

True happiness consists not in the multitude of friends, but in their worth and choice. — Ben Jonson

We are advertis'd by our loving friends. — William Shakespeare

What we say is important, my friend, for in most cases the mouth speaks what the heart is full of. — Jim Beggs

When friends ask, there is no tomorrow. — Proverb

You can't microwave a deep friendship. It takes time. Like yeast in dough, it takes time for openness and authenticity to permeate our core, but like baked bread, the aroma and taste is well worth the wait. — Chuck Tompkins

From the Mouths of Babes

Advice from a child playing physician: "Take this prescription to any grandma and get some milk and cookies." — Bob Thaves

Classmate of great-grandson Nicholas, commenting on Easter: "The Easter bunny died on the cross."

Do Easter bunnies have snow shoes?

Eight-year-old great-grandson Nicholas, blind from birth, describing a sailing adventure on Adirondack Lake: "The music of sunshine was in my face."

Grandson Caleb's interpretation of the Christmas carol: *Gloria in excelsis Deo*: "Gloria in egg shells a day old."

Out of the mouths of babes come words we shouldn't have said in the first place. — Jacob M. Braude

Two-year-old son Raymond, trying to say *Susquehanna River* as we drove along its banks: "Squash-a-banana River."

Young grandson Caleb, walking down driveway with potholes filled with water, replying to my request not to walk in the water: "But Grammee, my feets just go that way."

Gems

A burden shared is a burden lightened. — Unknown

A certain amount of opposition is a great help to man. Kites rise against, not with, the wind. — John Neal

A Christless Christmas is like a counterfeit dollar. — *ODB*, November 2001.

A chuckle a day may not keep the doctor away, but it sure does make those times in life's waiting room a little more bearable. —Anne Wilson Schaef

A critic is a person who knows the route but can't drive the car. — *Country*, December/January 2006, p. 4.

After about meal #25,000, the fun is gone.

A gem cannot be polished without friction, nor can we be perfected without trial. — *ODB*, September 2003.

A good life is like a good watch:
- open face
- busy hands
- pure as crystal
- full of good works
>   — Unknown

A gossip is a person with a keen sense of rumor. — Unknown

A halo has to fall only a few inches to become a noose. — Unknown

A hug is a perfect gift—one size fits all, and nobody minds if you give it back. — *Country*, December/January 2006, p. 23.

A human being has a natural desire to have more of a good thing than he needs. — Mark Twain

A hypocrite is a person who is not himself on Sunday. — *ODB*, October 2000.

A lie can travel halfway around the world while the truth is putting on its shoes. — Mark Twain

A little encouragement can spark a great accomplishment. — *ODB*, July 2001.

A negative attitude is like a flat tire. You're not going far until you change it. — Unknown

A people that values its privileges above its principles soon loses both. — Dwight D. Eisenhower

A person of integrity has nothing to hide. — *ODB*, October 2002.

A pessimist complains about the wind. The optimist expects it to change. The realist adjusts the sails. — William Arthur Ward

A plump wife and a big barn never did any man harm. — Rural Pearl, *Country*, December/January 2006, p. 68.

A rumor is as hard to unspread as butter. — Unknown

A rumor without a leg to stand on will get around some other way. — John Tudor

A smile adds a great deal to face value. — Unknown

A smile is a curve that can set things straight. — *ODB*, June 2005.

A son in college wrote home, saying, "$chool is really great. I am making lot$ of friend$ and $tudying hard. Plea$e $end me a card a$ I would love to hear from you. Love, your $on." The father wrote back, "I kNOw you are an hoNOr student, but do NOt forget that the pursuit of kNOwledge is a NOble task. You can never study eNOugh. Love, Dad." — David Jeremiah

A stitch in time saves nine. — English Proverb

A true measure of your worth includes all the benefits others have gained from your success. — Cullen Hightower

A voice like an audible toothache. — Ben Bova

A wise man changes his mind, but a fool never does. — Unknown

Advice is like cooking. You should try it before you feed it to others. — Herbert Browne

After all is said and done, more is said than done. — *ODB*, April 2001.

Age does not diminish the extreme disappointment of having a scoop of ice cream fall from the cone. — Jim Feibig

Age is only a matter of mind; if you don't mind, it doesn't matter. — Mark Twain

Always bear in mind that your own resolution to succeed is more important than any one thing. — Abraham Lincoln

Always do right. This will gratify some people and astonish the rest. — Mark Twain

Always listen to experts. They'll tell you what can't be done and why. Then do it. — Robert A. Heinlein

Always remember that you are absolutely unique—just like everyone else. — Margaret Mead

Always remember that we pass this way but once ... unless your spouse is reading the road map. — *Country*, December/January 2006, p. 60.

Always shoot for the moon. If you should fail and fall short, you'll still land among the stars. — Les Brown

An expert is a person who has made all the mistakes that can be made in a very narrow field. — Niels Bohr

An onion can make people cry, but there has never been a vegetable invented to make them laugh. — Will Rogers (prior to *Veggie Tales*)

And God created wrinkles. — Jane Mall

Anyone who thinks he knows all the answers isn't up-to-date on the questions. — Robert M. Miller, *The Best of RMM*, 1:97.

April hath put a spirit of youth in everything. — William Shakespeare

Are you between a rock and a hard place? Take refuge in the Rock of Ages. — *ODB*, October 2002.

Artificial intelligence is no match for natural stupidity. — Mortimer B. Zuckerman, "Words to Live By," *U.S. News & World Report*, January 2006.

As dead flies give perfume a bad smell, so a little folly outweighs wisdom and honor. — Ecclesiastes 10:1.

As light overcomes darkness, goodness can overcome evil. — *ODB*, March 2002.

As you go through life, concentrate on the roses instead of the thorns. — *ODB*, May 2003.

A word from your mouth speaks volumes about your heart. — *ODB*, May 2006.

Be a grace-giver, not a faultfinder. — *ODB*, July 2002.

Be kind to your friends—if it weren't for them, you would be a total stranger. — Unknown

Be sure you have more behind the counter than you put on display. —Unknown

Behold the turtle! He makes progress only when he sticks his neck out. —James Bryant Conant

Better than counting your years is making your years count. — Unknown

Beware: competition can destroy companionship. — *ODB*, August 2002.

Burnout is a disease of the incorrectly committed. — Unknown

By the time your face clears up, your mind gets fuzzy. — Chuck Swindoll, *Growing Strong in the Seasons of Life*, p. 244.

Carry each other's burdens, and in this way you will fulfill the law of Christ. — Galatians 6:2.

Civilizations do not give out; they give in. In a society where anything goes, eventually, everything will. — John Underwood

Compassion never goes out of fashion. — *ODB*, July 2002.

Connection does much, but encouragement does more. — Johann Wolfgang von Goethe

Contentment is priceless. — *ODB*, May 2002.

Courtesy is the shortest distance between two people. — Unknown

Cultivate your own capabilities. Rabbits don't fly. Eagles don't swim. Ducks look funny trying to climb. Squirrels don't have feathers. Stop comparing. Enjoy being you! There's plenty of room in the forest. — Chuck Swindoll, *Growing Strong in the Seasons of Life*, p. 464.

Death is not a period—it's only a comma. — *ODB*, November 2005.

Dig where the gold is ... unless you just need some exercise. — John M. Capozzi

Diplomacy is the art of letting other people have your way. — Daniele Vare

Discontentment makes rich men poor; contentment makes poor men rich! — *ODB*, June 2000.

Do not answer a fool according to his folly, lest you also be like him. — Proverbs 26:4.

Do not expect others to do for you what God has given you the ability to do for yourself. — Unknown

Don't be pushed by your problems; be led by your dreams. — Unknown

Don't complain about growing old; this privilege is denied many people. — *Country*, December/January 2006, p. 58.

Don't drive your stakes too deep—we're moving in the morning. — *ODB*, July 2003, April 2006.

Don't find a fault—find a remedy. — *ODB*, August 2005.

Don't go around saying the world owes you a living. The world owes you nothing. It was here first. — Mark Twain

Don't just live and let live, but live and help live. — Unknown

Don't think there are no crocodiles because the water is calm. — Malayan Proverb, *Country*, August/September 2006, p. 60.

Don't weary yourself trying to unscrew the inscrutable. — Chuck Swindoll, *Growing Deep in the Christian Life*, p. 101.

Eat the meat and leave the bones. — Unknown

Enjoy life, this is not a dress rehearsal. — Unknown

Enjoy the little things. One day you may look back and realize they were the big things. —Robert Brault

Even a bed of roses has thorns. — Unknown

Even if you're on the right track, you'll get run over if you just sit there. — Will Rogers

Even Moses was once a basket case. — Church sign

Every problem contains the seed of its own solution. — Norman Vincent Peale

Every time you speak, your mind is on parade. — *ODB*, June 2005.

Experience is like drawing without an eraser. — *Country*, December/January 2006, p. 57.

Familiarity breeds contempt—and children. — Mark Twain

Families are like fudge; mostly sweet with a few nuts. — Unknown

Feeding on God's truth will keep you from swallowing a lie. — *ODB*, April 2002.

Few people travel the road to success without a puncture or two. — *Country*, December/January 2006, p. 5.

Fire refines gold; adversity refines man. — *ODB*, October 2002.

First class is being alive and interested and different from everyone else. — Jane Mall

First learn the meaning of what you say, and then speak. — *Country*, December/January 2006, p. 43.

For every minute you are angry, you lose sixty seconds of happiness. — *ODB*, February 2005.

For fast-acting relief, try slowing down. —Lily Tomlin

Forgiveness is the perfume that the trampled flower casts back upon the foot that crushed it. — Unknown

Free cheese is only found in mousetraps. — Russian Proverb

Freedom always comes with a price. — *ODB*, May 2002.

Frustration is not having anyone to blame but yourself. — Unknown

Gentlemen, we are surrounded by insurmountable opportunities. — Pogo

God calls us to get into the game, not to keep score. — *ODB*, December 2002.

God can mend your broken heart, but you must give Him all the pieces. — *ODB*, September 2002.

God can turn any difficulty into an opportunity. — *ODB*, October 2001.

God does not shield us from life's storms; He shelters us in life's storms. — *ODB*, September 2002.

God doesn't expect us to do everything. — Unknown

God is more interested in our motives than our methods. — *ODB*, May 2002.

God is the friend of silence. Trees, flowers, grass grow in silence. See the stars, moon, and sun, how they move in silence. — Mother Teresa

God provides the armor, but we must put it on. — *ODB*, January 2003.

God takes us into His darkroom to develop our character. — *ODB*, July 2000.

God, who knows our load limit, graciously limits our load. — *ODB*, November 2002.

God will either lighten our load or strengthen our backs. — Croft M. Pentz, *1001 Things Your Mother Told You: And You Should Have Listened*, p. 121.

Golf is a good walk spoiled. — Mark Twain

Golf isn't a game; it's a choice that one makes with one's life. — Charles Rosin

Good communication is as stimulating as black coffee and just as hard to sleep after. — Anne Morrow Lindbergh

Gratitude is born in hearts that take time to count up past mercies. — Charles E. Jefferson

Great oak trees started out as little nuts that held their ground. — Unknown

"Grow up" is what the young are told; "age gracefully" when growing old. — *ODB*, July 2005.

Guard well within yourself that treasure, kindness. Know how to give without hesitation, how to lose without regret, how to acquire without meanness. — George Sand

Guts = grace under pressure. — Ernest Hemingway

Half our life is spent trying to find something to do with the time we have rushed through life trying to save. — Will Rogers

Hang on to your dignity because, if you have it, you have earned it. — Jane Mall

Happiness depends on happenings; joy depends on Jesus. — *ODB*, February 2003, July 2005.

Happiness is like a potato salad—when you share it with others, it's a picnic. — *Country*, December/January 2006, p. 20.

Happiness isn't getting what you want; it's wanting what you have. — Garth Brooks

Hardship is when we have to do without things our grandparents never heard of. — Unknown

He that can have patience can have what he will. — Benjamin Franklin

He that is good for making excuses is seldom good for anything else. — Benjamin Franklin

He who does what he should will not have time to do what he should not. — Unknown

Hold tightly what is eternal; hold lightly what is temporal. — *ODB*, March 2002.

Hope can be ignited by a spark of encouragement. — *ODB*, September 2002.

Hope in the heart puts a smile on the face. — *ODB*, November 2001.

Horse sense is stable thinking coupled with the ability to say "nay." — Unknown

Horse sense is the thing a horse has which keeps it from betting on people. — W. C. Fields

Hospitality can fill the emptiness of a lonely heart. — *ODB*, August 2002.

Housework is like stringing beads without a knot in the end of the string. — Suzanne Hye

Housework is something you do that nobody notices unless you don't do it. — Unknown

Humor may be defined as the kindly contemplation of the incongruities of life, and the artistic expression thereof. — Stephen Leacock

I am no longer young enough to know everything. — Oscar Wilde

I find the greatest thing in this world is not so much where we stand as in what direction we are moving. — Oliver Wendell Holmes

I hate being old!? You should love it—think of the alternative. — Unknown

I never get lost. Everyone tells me where to go. — Robert M. Miller, *The Best of RMM*, 1:63.

I am not one of those who in expressing opinions confine themselves to facts. — Mark Twain

I'll match my flops with anybody's but I wouldn't have missed 'em. Flops are a part of life's menu, and I've never been a girl to miss out on any of the courses. — Rosalind Russell

If a man is lazy, the rafters sag; if his hands are idle, the house leaks. — Ecclesiastes 10:18.

If a man has enough horse sense to treat his wife like a thoroughbred, she will never turn into an old nag. — Wisdom from Grandpa

If God had a refrigerator, your picture would be on it. — *ODB*, May 2002.

If it wasn't for the hot water the tea kettle wouldn't sing. — Unknown

If it's not broken, don't fix it. If it starts to break, fix it quick. — Old adage

If life is a grind, use it to sharpen your character. — *ODB*, November 2003.

If tears should fall, they're settling the dust—that's all. — Ruth Bell Graham

If you are out of a job—that's depression. If I am out of a job—that's a tragedy. — Jo Petty, *Bits of Silver and Gold, Love.*

If you are in tune with heaven, you'll have a song in your heart. — *ODB*, June 2001.

If you are patient in one moment of anger, you will escape a hundred days of sorrow. — Chinese Proverb

If you can't convince them—confuse them. — Robert M. Miller, *The Best of RMM*, 1:73.

If you find a path with no obstacles, it probably doesn't lead anywhere. — Frank A. Clark

If you live to be a hundred, you've got it made. Very few people die past that age. — George Burns

If you pause to think, you'll find cause to thank. — *ODB*, April 2002.

If you remove the rocks, the brook would lose its song. — Unknown

If you see people without a smile today, give them one of yours. — *ODB*, April 2002.

If you tell the truth you don't have to remember anything. — Mark Twain

If you think education is expensive, try ignorance. — Derek Bok

If you wait for perfect conditions, you'll never get anything done. — Ecclesiastes 4:11 (paraphrased).

If you want to save face, keep the lower half shut. — Ann Landers

If you want to walk on water, you've got to get out of the boat. — John Ortberg

If you watch a game, it's fun. If you play it, it's recreation. If you work at it, it's golf. — Bob Hope

If your head is made out of butter, don't sit near the fire. — Martin Luther

If your mind goes blank, don't forget to turn off the sound. — *ODB*, July 2003.

In mentally picking flaws in others, I pick a worse flaw in myself. — Jo Petty, *Bits of Silver and Gold, Love.*

It infuriates me to be wrong when I know I'm right. — Molière

It is a funny thing about life; if you refuse to accept anything but the best, you very often get it. — W. Somerset Maugham

It is better to wear out than rust out. — Bishop Richard Cumberland

It is better to be faithful than to be out in front. — *ODB*, April 2002.

It is good to let a little sunshine out as well as in. — Church sign

It is never too late to start doing what is right! — Chuck Swindoll, *Growing Deep in the Christian Life*, p. 380.

It isn't necessary to blow out another person's light in order to let your light shine. — *Country*, December/January 2006, p. 63.

It isn't our position that makes us happy, but rather our disposition. — Unknown

It paints my simple spirit with tints of majesty. — Emily Dickinson

It's a lot easier to stay out of trouble than to get out of trouble. — Unknown

It's amazing what can be accomplished when you don't care who gets the credit. — *ODB*, March 2005.

It's better to keep your mouth closed and be thought a fool than to open it and remove all doubt. — Mark Twain

It's easier to build a boy than it is to mend a man. — Charles Gavin

It's hard to hate someone when you're complimenting him. — *ODB*, June 2002.

It's nice to be important, but it's more important to be nice. — John Cassis

It's not the bad days that get you down, but the good ones that you missed. — Unknown

It's risky to go out on a limb—but that's where the fruit is. — *ODB*, January 2003.

It's what you learn after you know it all that counts. — John Wooden

Just because everything is different, it doesn't mean anything has changed. — Irene Porter

Just because it's old doesn't mean it's good. — Jane Mall

Keep away from people who try to belittle your ambitions. Small people always do that, but the really great make you feel that you, too, can become great. — Mark Twain

Kind criticism is always the right kind. — *ODB*, June 2002.

Kind words can be short and easy to speak, but their echoes are truly endless. — Mother Teresa

Kindness is a language that the deaf can hear and the blind can see. — Mark Twain

Kindness to the elderly brightens their sunset years. — *ODB*, June 2003.

Laughter is an instant vacation. — Milton Berle, *Country*, August/September 2006, p. 64

Learn to listen. Opportunity sometimes knocks very softly. — H. Jackson Brown, Jr.

Let the words I speak today be soft and tender, for tomorrow I may have to eat them. — Unknown

Let us look to our own circumstances as we do to our hands, to see if they be dirty. — Florence Nightingale

Life is 10 percent what happens to us and 90 percent how we respond. — Chuck Swindoll

Life is like a game of tennis—you can't win without serving well. — *ODB*, April 2001.

Life is like an onion. You peel away a layer at a time, and sometimes you cry. — Carl Sandburg

Life is like a coin. You can spend it anyway you care, but you can spend it only once! — Lillian Dickson

Life is like a grindstone. Whether it polishes or grinds you down depends on what you're made of. — *Country*, December/January 2006, p. 21.

Life is like a ten-speed bike. Most of us have gears we never use. — Charles M. Schultz

Life is uncertain—eat dessert first. — *Country*, December/January 2006, p. 59.

Like two old shoes; a little worn but comfortable. — Jane Mall

Listen with your heart. Your ears can deceive you. — Unknown

Living in the past has one thing in its favor—it's cheaper. — Unknown

Lord, fill my mouth with worthwhile stuff, and nudge me when I've said enough. — Unknown

Luck is a matter of preparation meeting opportunity. — Oprah Winfrey

Man is not great till he beholds his own smallness. — Unknown

Manners are the happy way of doing things. — Ralph Waldo Emerson

Many people are lonely because they build walls instead of bridges. — *ODB*, January 2001.

Middle age is when the broadness of mind and the narrowness of the waist change places. — Mortimer B. Zuckerman, "Words to Live By," *U.S. News & World Report*, January 2006.

Minds are like parachutes; they only function when open. — T. Dewar

My mother's menu consisted of two choices; take it or leave it.

Never fear criticism when you're right; never ignore it when you're wrong. — *ODB*, November 2003.

Never give the devil a ride—he will always want to drive. — Church sign

Never put off until tomorrow what you can do the day after tomorrow. — Mark Twain

Never regret growing old; many are denied that privilege. — Unknown

Never throw dirt. You only lose ground. — Unknown

No act of kindness, no matter how small, is ever wasted. — Aesop

No day is over if it makes a memory. — Unknown

No matter how much frosting you put on a bad cake, it's still a bad cake. — Unknown

No one is ever out of work if he minds his own business. — Unknown

No sword bites so fiercely as an evil tongue. — Sir Philip Sidney

Nobody cares that you walked ten miles to school (uphill both ways)—in the snow—with no shoes. — Jane Mall

Not many really creative people—in the process of creating—keep everything neat, picked up, and in its place. — Chuck Swindoll, *Stress Fractures*, p. 161.

Nothing enters the brain through the open mouth. — Unknown

Nothing is a waste of time if you use the experience wisely. — Auguste Rodin

Nothing makes a person more productive than the last minute. — Unknown

Nothing splendid has ever been achieved except by those who dared believe that something inside them was superior to circumstance. — Bruce Barton

Old age is not a time to coast but to climb. — *ODB*, December 2001.

Old age is like everything else—to make it a success, you have to start young. — *Country*, December/January 2006, p. 61.

One of the most difficult things to give away is kindness. It is usually returned. — Cort R. Flint

Only a fool tests the depth of the water with both feet. — African Proverb

Opportunities to be kind are never hard to find. — *ODB*, July2003, May 2005.

Other things may change us, but we start and end with family. — Anthony Brandt

Others won't care how much we know until they know how much we care. — Chuck Swindoll, *Come Before Winter*, p. 261.

Our life is what our thoughts make it. — James Allen

Our mirrors reflect the outward appearance; God's mirror reveals the inward condition. — *ODB*, July 2006.

Our opinions do not really blossom into fruition until we have expressed them to someone else. — Mark Twain

Our tongue can be our own worst enemy. — *ODB*, October 2005.

Our words and our deeds should speak the same language. — *ODB*, August 2002.

Overheard at a wedding reception: "They make a wonderful couple. He's a hypochondriac, and she's a pill." — Ann Landers

Painting is easy when you don't know how, but very difficult when you do. — Edgar Degas

Patience is the ability to idle your motor when you feel like stripping your gears. — Barbara Johnson, *Where Does a Mother Go to Resign?*

People from the past can give us pointers for the present. — *ODB*, August 2002.

People will listen to you carefully if they see you living faithfully. — *ODB*, June 2005.

Pleasure lies in the heart, not in the happenstance. — Luci Swindoll

Poverty of purpose is far worse than poverty of purse. — *ODB*, July 2005.

Practice what you preach until you are good at it. Then shut your mouth and set a good example. — Unknown

Praise is the voice of a soul set free. — *ODB*, September 2005.

Pray for a good harvest, but keep on hoeing. — *ODB*, May 2001.

Prediction is very difficult, especially about the future. — Niels Bohr

Procrastination is the assassination of motivation. — Unknown

Remember, a diamond is nothing more than a piece of coal that has been hard-pressed a long time. — Unknown

Remember, it takes both the rain and the sunshine to make a rainbow. — Unknown

Rumor travels faster, but it don't stay put as long as truth. — Will Rogers

Sacrifice is the true measure of generosity. — Jason Hurst

See what will happen if you don't stop biting your fingernails? — Will Rogers, to his niece, on seeing the Venus de Milo.

Senior citizens = "Great Grays." — Unknown

Seven days without laughter make one weak. — Joel Goodman

Some cause happiness wherever they go; others whenever they go. — Oscar Wilde

Some people are like blisters. They never appear until the work is done. — *Country*, December/January 2006, p. 62.

Some people go through life standing at the complaint counter. — *ODB*, May 2006.

Some people, no matter how old they get, never lose their beauty. They just move it from their faces to their hearts. — Martin Buxbaum

Some troubles come from wanting our own way; others come from being allowed to have it. — *ODB*, October 2000.

Sometimes we must step apart from the world to find our place in it. — Unknown

Sometimes when we are generous in small, barely detectable ways it can change someone else's life forever. — Margaret Cho

Spring is nature's way of saying "Let's party!" — Robin Williams

Statistics are no substitute for judgment. — Henry Clay

Success comes in cans; I can, you can, we can. — Unknown

Success in life comes not from holding a good hand, but in playing a poor hand well. — Denis Waitley

Success is built on the ability to do better than good enough. — Unknown

Success is getting what you want. Happiness is wanting what you get. — Dale Carnegie

Success is not a destination; it is a journey. — Ben Sweetland

Success means that you get up one more time than you fall down. — *ODB*, April 2001.

Success without a successor is failure. — John Maxwell

Success without honor is an unseasoned dish; it will satisfy your hunger, but it won't taste good. — Joe Paterno

Such is the human race; often it does seem a pity that Noah and his party didn't miss the boat. — Mark Twain

Sunset in one land is sunrise in another. — *ODB*, July 2005.

Sympathy is two hearts tugging at one load. — *ODB*, January 2001, March 2002.

Tact is the ability to make a point without making an enemy. — *ODB*, July 2005.

Tact is the art of making guests feel at home when that's really where you wish they were. — George E. Bergman

Tell me and I'll forget; show me and I may remember; involve me and I'll understand. — Chinese Proverb; *Country*, December/January 2006, p. 27.

Thank God for dirty dishes,
They have a tale to tell.
While others may go hungry,
We're eating very well.
        — Unknown

The best gifts are tied with heartstrings. — *ODB*, December 2000.

The best portion of a good man's life, his little, nameless, unremembered acts of kindness and of love. — William Wadsworth

The best time to stop a fight is before it starts. — *ODB*, May 2002.

The best way to cheer yourself is to try to cheer someone else up. — Mark Twain

The best way to judge an individual is by observing how he treats people who can do him absolutely no good. — Ann Landers

The difference between the impossible and the possible lies in a person's determination. — Tommy Lasorda

The difference between the right word and the almost right word is the difference between lightning and a lightning bug. — Mark Twain

The files of heaven are filled with stories of redeemed, refitted renegades and rebels. — Chuck Swindoll, *Growing Strong in the Seasons of Life*, p. 373.

The fly that buzzes loudest usually gets swatted first. — *ODB*, May 2005.

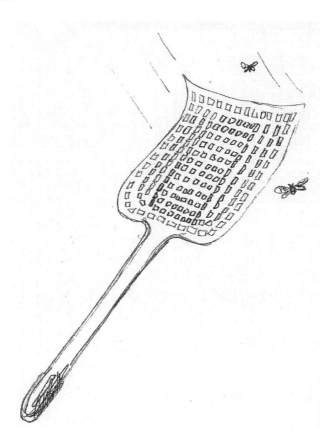

The grass is always greener over the septic tank. — Erma Bombeck

The heart of a wise inclines to the right, but the heart of the fool to the left. —Ecclesiastes 10:2.

The human race has one really effective weapon, and that is laughter. — Mark Twain

The hypocrite has God on his tongue and the world in his heart. — *ODB*, July 2002.

The important thing about your lot in life is whether you use it for parking or building. — Unknown

The lowest ebb is the turn of the tide. — Henry Wadsworth Longfellow

The man who cannot forget is worse than he who cannot remember. — Unknown

The more the words, the less the meaning. — Ecclesiastes 6:12.

The most important thing in communications is to hear what isn't being said. — Peter F. Drucker

The most perfect technique is that which is not noticed at all. — Pablo Casals

The most severe violence in our society is caused by ignorance. — Ellen Goldman

The only difference between stumbling blocks and stepping-stones is the way you use them. — Adriana Doyle

The only thing wrong with doing nothing is that you never know when you are finished. — Unknown

The only time people dislike gossip is when you gossip about them. — Will Rogers

The only way to keep from making mistakes is to do nothing—and that's the greatest mistake of all. — Unknown

The person who refuses to hear criticism has no chance to learn from it. — *ODB*, May 2006.

The person who rows the boat generally doesn't have time to rock it. — Unknown

The pessimist sees the difficulty in every opportunity; the optimist sees the opportunity in every difficulty. — Winston Churchill

The report of my death was an exaggeration. — Mark Twain

The room for improvement is a room never full. — Unknown

The same fence that shuts others out shuts you in. — William Taylor Copeland

The soul would have no rainbow if the eyes had no tears. — *ODB*, September 2003.

The storms of our life prove the strength of our anchor. — *ODB*, March 2002.

The stronger the winds, the deeper the roots, and the longer the winds, the more beautiful the tree. — Chuck Swindoll, *Growing Strong in the Seasons of Life*, p. 436.

The sun sets early for those who live in the valley. — Unknown

The time is always right to do what is right. — Martin Luther King, Jr.

The tongue, being in a wet place, is apt to slip. — *ODB*, October 2002.

The trouble with talking too fast is you may say something you haven't thought of yet. — Ann Landers

The true measure of a person is what's in the heart. — *ODB*, June 2005.

The way to stop a loud argument is by a soft-spoken word. — Chuck Swindoll, *Come Before Winter*, p. 303.

The weariest river winds somewhere safe to sea. — Algernon Charles Swinburne

The world breaks everyone, and afterward many are strong in the broken places. — Ernest Hemingway

There ain't no surer way to find out whether you like people or hate them than to travel with them. — Mark Twain

There are two ways a man can learn; one by experience, the other by expense. — Unknown

There are hundreds of languages in the world, but a smile speaks all of them. — Unknown

There are no gains without pains. — *ODB*, August 2005.

There are no shortcuts to any place worth going. — Beverly Sills

There is no tranquilizer in the world more effective than a few kind words. — Unknown

There is nothing so strong as gentleness; nothing so gentle as real strength. — St. Francis de Sales

> There is so much good in the worst of us,
> And so much bad in the best of us,
> That it hardly behooves any of us,
> To talk about the rest of us.
> — Edward Wallis Hoch

There's no limit to the good you can do if you don't care who gets the credit. — *ODB*, March 2002.

There's plenty of room at the top. There's just no room to sit down. — Unknown

There are five kinds of broken things in this world.
- There's the kind which when they are broken, can never be fixed.
- Then there's the kind that'll fix themselves if you leave them alone.
- There's the kind which are none of my business. Somebody else has got to fix them.
- There's the kind which when they are broken, you should never worry about—them only God can fix.
- And then there's the kind I got to fix. That's what I'm doing. Fixin' this gate. — Charlie W. Shedd

They call you stubborn when you fail but persistent when you succeed. — Mortimer B. Zuckerman, "Words to Live By," *U.S. News & World Report*, January 2006.

They laughed their bones loose. — Mark Twain

Think before you act; think twice before you speak. — *ODB*, May 2001.

Those that criticize the most are those that create nothing. — Chuck Swindoll

Those who follow the crowd soon become part of the crowd. — *ODB*, November 2003.

Those who get too big for their britches will be exposed in the end. — Unknown

Those who listen to lies lose the ability to hear the truth. — *ODB*, June 2003.

Time and tide wait for no man. — Geoffrey Chaucer

Time may be a great healer, but it's a terrible makeup artist. — *Country*, December/January 2006, p. 64.

To avoid being tempted by forbidden fruit, stay away from the devil's orchard. — *ODB*, November 2003.

To avoid lying, do nothing that needs a cover-up. — *ODB*, June 2002.

To handle a hard situation, try a soft answer. — *ODB*, January 2001.

To laugh is to be fully human. — *ODB*, August 2005.

To lose is not always failure. — *ODB*, June 2002.

To me old age is always fifteen years older than I am. — Bernard Baruch

To rule your tongue, let Christ reign in your heart. — *ODB*, July 2002.

To spend time wisely, invest in eternity. — *ODB*, April 2002.

To understand a man, you must know his memories. The same is true of a nation. — Anthony Quale

Today's thoughts become tomorrow's actions, which become next week's habits, which become next year's character. — Unknown

Tough times teach trust. — *ODB*, July 2002.

True service is love in working clothes. — *ODB*, July 2006.

Trust your hunches. They're usually based on facts filed away just below the conscious level. — Dr. Joyce Brothers

Unhappy is the person who knows it all—and has no one to tell it to. — Robert M. Miller, *The Best of RMM*, 2:21.

Unless we're humble, we're sure to stumble. — *ODB*, June 2003.

Utopia is the good old days, plus all the modern conveniences. — Thomas F. Shubnell

Velvet-lined trap. — Unknown

We can't all be heroes because somebody has to sit on the curb and clap as they go by. — Will Rogers

We cannot avoid growing old, but we can avoid growing cold. — *ODB*, January 2002.

We cannot direct the wind, but we can adjust the sails. — Bertha Calloway

We do not remember days. We remember moments. — Cesare Pavese

We have different gifts, according to the grace given us. — Romans 12:6

We never retire from being useful to God. — *ODB*, June 2002.

What the mind of man can conceive and believe, it can achieve. — Napoleon Hill

What we are when we are old is what we learned when we were young. — Unknown

What we call adversity, God calls opportunity. — *ODB*, January 2002.

What we obtain too cheap, we esteem too lightly. — Thomas Paine

What we say reveals who we are. — *ODB*, June 2002.

What you are speaks so loudly I can't hear what you say. — Ralph Waldo Emerson

What you want others to become—you yourself must be. — Unknown

When a habit begins to cost money, it's called a hobby. — *Country*, December/January 2006, p. 65.

When a man gets too big for his breeches, his hat won't fit either. — Unknown

When all else fails, read the instructions. — Agnes Allen

When I criticize you—that's constructive criticism. When you criticize me—that's destructive criticism. — Jo Petty, *Bits of Silver and Gold, Love.*

When offended, don't respond in kind; respond with kindness. — *ODB*, May 2002.

When temptation knocks, send Jesus to the door. — *ODB*, October 2001.

When the elephants fight, it's the grass that suffers. — African Proverb

When there are troubles around me, I make certain they aren't inside me. — Unknown

When we forget our priorities, we argue about trivialities. — *ODB*, October 2002.

When you are right, no one remembers. When you are wrong, no one forgets. — Irish Proverb

When you are swept off your feet, land on your knees. — *ODB*, July 2002.

When you bury the hatchet, don't mark the grave. — Church sign

When you can't sleep, don't count sheep. Talk to the Shepherd. — *ODB*, March 2001.

When you encourage someone, both of your loads will be lighter. — *ODB*, March 2002.

When you lash out at others, you're sure to hurt yourself. — *ODB*, April 2001.

When you're over the hill, you start picking up speed. — Charles M. Schultz, *Peanuts Wisdom*.

When you sing your own praise you are always out of tune. — *ODB*, June 2000.

When you turn green with envy you are ripe for trouble. — *ODB*, October 2002.

Wherever you go, there you are. — Jon Kabat-zinn

Whether a man winds up with a nest egg, or a goose egg, depends a lot on the kind of a chick he marries. — Wisdom from Grandpa

Whoever wants to reach a distant goal must take many small steps. — Helmut Schmidt

Why can't life's big problems come when we're teenagers and know everything? — Unknown

Why is it that we rejoice at a birth and grieve at a funeral? It is because we are not the person involved. — Mark Twain

Winners never quit, and quitters never win. — *ODB*, March 2002.

Wise is the listener who doesn't feel compelled to fill up all the blank spaces. — Chuck Swindoll, *Growing Strong in the Seasons of Life*, p. 90.

Wise men talk because they have something to say; fools because they have to say something. — Plato

Wise men talk about ideas, ordinary men talk about things, and fools talk about each other. — Unknown

Worry doesn't improve the future, it only ruins the present. — *ODB*, April 2001.

Worry is interest paid on trouble before it comes due. — *Country*, December/January 2006/2007, p. 22.

Worry is like a rocking chair—it will give you something to do, but it won't get you anywhere. — *ODB*, October 2000.

Wrinkles should merely indicate where the smiles have been. — Mark Twain

You can never bury your influence. — Church sign

You cannot prevent the birds of sorrow from flying over your head, but you can prevent them from building nests in your hair. — Chinese Proverb

You can sell your honor but you can't buy it back. — Unknown

You can't get race horses out of mules. — Unknown

You can't rid yourself of a bad temper by losing it. — Roy V. Zuck, *The Speaker's Quote Book*, p. 13.

You can't shake hands with a clenched fist. — Indira Gandhi

You can't trust Satan's cease-fires. — Chuck Swindoll, *The Quest for Character*, p. 24.

You cannot depend on your eyes when your imagination is out of focus. — Mark Twain

You cannot teach what you do not know, nor lead where you do not go. — *ODB*, September 2005.

Lois E. Scott

You have one tongue and two ears – use them in that ratio. — Joel H. Weldon

You're not famous until your mother knows about it. — Jay Leno

You're only cooking up trouble when you stew about tomorrow. — *ODB*, December 2005.

Your parents brought you up; don't let them down. — *ODB*, June 2001.

Giving

Be as gracious in receiving as you are in giving. — *ODB*, April 2002.

Be charitable before wealth makes thee covetous. — Sir Thomas Browne

Charity begins at home. — Terence

Charity sees the need, not the cause. — German Proverb

Generosity is like a rare gem. Not many of us possess it, but when it is seen it sparkles. — Chuck Swindoll, *Growing Strong in the Seasons of Life*, p. 406.

Giving is a joy. We should think, "What can I share?" not "What can I spare?" — Esther Baldwin York

Giving is a necessity sometimes; more urgent, indeed, than having. — Margaret Lee Runbeck

It is in giving that we receive. — Jo Petty, *Bits of Silver and Gold, Love.*

It is more blessed to give than to receive. — Jesus, Acts 21:35.

No person was ever honored for what he received. Honor has been the reward for what he gave. — Calvin Coolidge

Sacrifice is the true measure of our giving. — *ODB*, March 2003.

Lois E. Scott

The best thing to give to your enemy is forgiveness; to an opponent, tolerance; to a friend, your heart; to your child, a good example; to a father, deference; to your mother, conduct that will make her proud of you; to yourself, respect; to all men, charity. — Francis Maitland Balfour

Those who give generously have more than those who hoard. — Chuck Swindoll, *Come Before Winter*, p. 303.

We haven't learned to live until we've learned to give. — *ODB*, September 2003.

We make a living by what we earn; we make a life by what we give. — *ODB*, March 2002.

We may give without loving, but we cannot love without giving. — *ODB*, February 2002.

God, Jesus Christ,
and the Holy Spirit

All creation points to the almighty Creator. — *ODB*, August 2005.

All I have seen teaches me to trust God for all I have not seen. — Ralph Waldo Emerson

Also I heard the voice of the Lord, saying: "Whom shall I send, and who will go for Us?" Then I said, "Here I am! Send me." — Isaiah 6:8.

As God adds years to your life, ask Him to add life to your years. — *ODB*, March 2002.

Because Jesus has risen from the dead, He has the last word in life and death. — *ODB*, August 2006.

But the fruit of the Spirit is love, joy, peace, longsuffering, kindness, goodness, faithfulness, gentleness, self-control. Against such there is no law. — Galatians 5:22–23.

Christ can transform painful trials into glorious triumphs. — *ODB*, November 2003.

Christ creates unity in the midst of diversity. — *ODB*, August 2002.

Christ departed so that the Holy Spirit could be imparted. — *ODB*, May 2003.

Christ is not asking for our vote but for our life. — Jo Petty, *Bits of Silver and Gold, Love.*

Christ is the greatest gift known to man. — *ODB*, March 2002.

Christ paid a debt He didn't owe to satisfy a debt we couldn't pay. — *ODB*, 2003.

Christ's resurrection is cause for our celebration. — *ODB*, September 2005.

Christianity is truly a voluntary commitment. — Jo Petty, *Bits of Silver and Gold, Love.*

Even youths grow tired and weary, and young men stumble and fall; but those who hope in the Lord will renew their strength. They will soar on wings like eagles; they will run and not grow weary, they will walk and not be faint. — Isaiah 40:30–31.

Every loss leaves a space that only God's presence can fill. — *ODB*, August 2005.

Everyone must face God as Savior or as Judge. — *ODB*, September 2006.

Go home to your friends, and tell them what great things the Lord has done for you. — Mark 5:19.

God does not ask us to go where He does not lead. — *ODB*, July 2003.

God is never late; but He sure does miss opportunities to be early. — Unknown

God is not a vending machine. — *ODB*, June 2003.

God knows your telephone number. — Anthony Burger

God made me fast; and when I run, I feel His pleasure. — Eric Liddell

God uses ordinary people to carry out His extraordinary plan. — *ODB*, August 2003, November 2003.

God uses ordinary people to do extraordinary work. — *ODB*, January 2003.

God uses our difficulties to develop our character. — *ODB*, February 2003.

God walks with us. He scoops us up in His arms or simply sits with us in silent strength until we cannot avoid the awesome recognition that yes, even now, He is there. — Gloria Gaither

God's timing is always right—wait patiently for Him. — *ODB*, October 2003.

He'll give you grace for the race. — Unknown

I am the vine; you are the branches. If a man remains in me and I in him, he will bear much fruit; apart from me you can do nothing. — John 15:5.

I have lived a long time; and the longer I live, the more convincing proofs I see of this truth—that God governs in the affairs of men. — Benjamin Franklin

I know God will not give me anything I can't handle. I just wish that He didn't trust me so much. — Mother Teresa

I may tremble on the Rock, but the Rock never trembles under me! — Chuck Swindoll, *Stress Fractures*, p. 267.

I tell you when the Spirit of God is on us for service, resting upon us, we are anointed, and then we can do great things. — Dwight L. Moody

If a man owns a hundred sheep, and one of them wanders away, will he not leave the ninety-nine on the hills and go to look for the one that wandered off? … In the same way your Father in heaven is not willing that any of these little ones should be lost. — Matthew 18:12, 14.

If you know Jesus, you'll never walk alone. — *ODB*, October 2003.

In nature we hear the voice of God. — *ODB*, August 2005.

Instead of looking at hypocrites, look at Jesus. — *ODB*, August 2003.

Jesus doesn't need lawyers, He needs witnesses. — *ODB*, June 2005.

Little things done in Christ's name are great things. — *ODB*, February 2003.

Nothing stays done, Lord. Nothing ever stays neat and clean or finished. And no one ever stays fed. But, Lord, You do the same thing every day—bringing the sun up, placing the clouds, darkening the sky at evening—yet Your work is done with such flair! — Unknown

Only Jesus can transform your life. — *ODB*, June 2005.

Only Living Water can quench the driving thirst of the soul. — *ODB*, August 2005.

Our only ground of victory over evil powers is our union with the Lord Jesus Christ. — Chuck Swindoll, *Stress Fractures*, p. 205.

Safety is not found in the absence of danger but in the presence of God. — *ODB*, October 2003.

Satan's number one weapon is pride. God's number one defense is humility. — Larry Burkett

The better you know Jesus in your heart, the more the world will see Jesus in your life. — *ODB*, September 2005.

The Christian's heart is the Holy Spirit's home. — *ODB*, August 2005.

The Great Physician is always on call. — *ODB*, April 2003.

The Great Physician always has the right remedy. — *ODB*, June 2005.

The lowly carpenter of Nazareth was the mighty architect of the universe. — *ODB*, March 2002.

The only leader worth following is one who is following Christ. — *ODB*, September 2005.

The resurrection of Jesus is a fact of history that demands a response of faith. — *ODB*, April 2003.

The straight and narrow way is God's way for a crooked generation. — *ODB*, June 2005.

The way to face Christ as Judge is to know Him as your Savior. — *ODB*, January 2003.

There is no true happiness apart from holiness, and no holiness apart from Christ. — *ODB*, September 2005.

To enjoy the future, accept God's forgiveness for the past. — *ODB*, August 2003.

To hear God's voice, turn down the world's volume. — *ODB*, August 2005.

To master temptation, let Christ master you. — *ODB*, October 2003.

To sing God's praise, keep your heart in tune with Him. — *ODB*, November 2003.

Unless God changes a person's heart, nothing lasting will be achieved. — Will Metzger

We are spiritually blind if we cannot see God's hand in nature. — *ODB*, April 2002.

We often praise the evening clouds, and tints so gay and bold; but seldom think upon our God, who tinged those clouds with gold. — Sir Walter Scott

What you decide about Jesus will determine your destiny. — *ODB*, September 2003.

What you do with Jesus now determines what He will do with you later. — *ODB*, August 2005.

When a Christian hits rock bottom, he finds that Christ is a firm foundation. — *ODB*, August 2005.

When God is ready to change a heart, it gets changed. No one is an "impossible case" to God. — Chuck Swindoll, *Growing Deep in the Christian Life*, pages 154–155.

When Jesus changes your heart, He gives you a heart for others. — *ODB*, June 2005.

When the wrappings and ribbons are in the trash, the manger scene is back in the attic, the friends and family have said good-bye, and the house feels empty and so do you—there is One who waits to fill your heart and renew your hope. — Chuck Swindoll, *Come Before Winter*, p. 214.

When you receive Christ, God's work in you has just begun. — *ODB*, August 2005.

Write your plans in pencil, then give God the eraser. — *ODB*, October 2003.

You don't need to know where you're going if you let God do the leading. — *ODB*, December 2003.

Government

A government big enough to give you everything you want, is strong enough to take everything you have. — Thomas Jefferson

As one small candle may light a thousand, so the light here kindled hath shone unto many, yea in some sort to our whole nation; let the glorious name of Jehovah have all the praise. — William Bradford, on the signing the *Mayflower Compact* aboard the *Mayflower*, November 11, 1620.

Be thankful we're not getting all the government we're paying for. — Will Rogers

Beware the greedy hand of government, thrusting itself into every corner and crevice of industry. — Thomas Paine

Educate and inform the whole mass of the people. They are the only sure reliance for the preservation of our liberty. — Thomas Jefferson

For every action there is an equal and opposite government program. — Bob Wells

He who builds a better mousetrap these days runs into material shortages, patent-infringement suits, work stoppages, collusive bidding, discount discrimination—and taxes. — H. E. Martz

I don't make jokes. I just watch the government and report the facts. — Will Rogers

If people let government decide what foods they eat and what medicines they take, their bodies will soon be in as sorry a state as are the souls of those who live under tyranny. — Thomas Jefferson

In my many years I have come to a conclusion that one useless man is a shame, two is a law firm, and three or more is a congress. — John Adams

It is the duty of the patriot to protect his country from his government. — Thomas Paine

Millions of laws, and not one improvement on the Ten Commandments. — Unknown

The government is like a baby's alimentary canal, with a happy appetite at one end and no responsibility at the other. — Ronald Reagan

The hardest thing in the world to understand is the income tax. — Albert Einstein

The income tax has made more liars out of the American people than golf has. — Will Rogers

There's a lot to be said for cabbage. The Lord's Prayer has fifty-six words. Lincoln's Gettysburg Address has 266. The Ten Commandments contain 297. The Declaration of Independence has three hundred. A government order setting the price of cabbage has 26,911. — Unknown

There's no trick to being a humorist when you have the whole government working for you. — Will Rogers

You know what's interesting about Washington? It's the kind of place where second-guessing has become second nature. — George W. Bush

Grace

But by the grace of God I am what I am. — Apostle Paul, 1 Corinthians 15:10.

For the law was given through Moses; grace and truth came through Jesus Christ. — John 1:17.

From the fullness of His grace we have all received one blessing after another. — John 1:16.

God gives grace just when we need it. — *ODB*, April 2002.

God's grace gives us what we don't deserve. — *ODB*, August 2002.

Grace is an unearned blessing given by God to an unworthy recipient. — *ODB*, August 2006.

Ground filled with the roots of bitterness needs to be plowed by the grace of God. — *ODB*, October 2004.

My grace is sufficient for you, for my power is made perfect in weakness. — Lord Jesus, to the Apostle Paul, 2 Corinthians 12:9.

No cosmetics for the face can compare with God's transforming grace. — *ODB*, May 2002.

The beauty of grace—our only permanent deliverance from guilt—is that it meets us where we are and gives us what we don't deserve. — Chuck Swindoll, *Stress Fractures*, p. 264.

The grace of our Lord Jesus be with you. — Romans 16:20.

Home

Home of Duane and Andrea Scott
by Marion Cardwell-Ferrer, Groton, NY

An old home is like the magic of an old violin. The music of the past is wrought into it. — Unknown

By wisdom a house is built, and through understanding it is established; through knowledge its rooms are filled with rare and beautiful treasures. — Proverbs 24:3-4.

Home is a lot of things, but mainly it is a place where life makes up its mind. — Unknown

Home is the bottom line of life, the anvil upon which attitudes and convictions are hammered out—the single most influential force in our earthly existence. — Chuck Swindoll, *Home: Where Life Makes Up Its Mind*, p. 5.

Home is where the heart can laugh without shyness and where the heart's tears can dry at their own pace. — Unknown

Like a bird that strays from its nest is a man who strays from his home. — Proverbs 27:8.

The right temperature at home is maintained by warm hearts, not hot heads. — Unknown

The wise woman builds her house, but with her own hands the foolish one tears hers down. — Proverbs 14:1.

Knowledge, Wisdom, Education, and Common Sense

A great teacher never strives to explain his vision—he simply invites you to stand beside him and see for yourself. — Rev. R. Inman

An ignorant person is one who doesn't know what you have just found out. — Will Rogers

Be curious always! For knowledge will not acquire you; you must acquire it. — Sudie Back

Common sense is genius dressed in its working clothes. — Ralph Waldo Emerson

Common sense is the collection of prejudices acquired by age eighteen. — Albert Einstein

Educate men without religion, and you make them but clever devils. — Arthur Wellesley, 1st Duke of Wellington

Education is learning what you didn't even know you didn't know. — Daniel J. Boorstin

Education: that which reveals to the wise, and conceals from the stupid, the vast limits of their knowledge. — Mark Twain

Education's purpose is to replace an empty mind with an open one. — Malcolm S. Forbes

Everyone gets so much information all day long that they lose their common sense. — Gertrude Stein

Facts are stubborn things, but statistics are more pliable. — Mark Twain

For the Lord gives wisdom, and from His mouth come knowledge and understanding. — Proverbs 2:6.

Gold there is, and rubies in abundance, but lips that speak knowledge are a rare jewel. — Proverbs 20:15.

He who works his land will have abundant food, but he who chases fantasies lacks judgment. — Proverbs 12:11.

How much better to get wisdom than gold, to choose understanding rather than silver. — Proverbs 16:16.

I never let my schooling interfere with my education. — Mark Twain

I'm always fascinated by the way memory diffuses fact. — Diane Sawyer

If you don't read the newspaper you are uninformed, if you do read the newspaper you are misinformed. — Mark Twain

Integrity without knowledge is weak and useless, and knowledge without integrity is dangerous and dreadful. — Samuel Johnson (1709–1784)

Listen to advice and accept instruction, and in the end you will be wise. — Proverbs 19:20.

Never mistake knowledge for wisdom. One helps you make a living; the other helps you make a life. — Sandra Carey

Nothing astonishes men so much as common sense and plain dealing. — Ralph Waldo Emerson

Stay away from a foolish man, for you will not find knowledge on his lips. — Proverbs 14:7.

Stupid is forever, ignorance can be fixed. — Don Wood

The fear of the Lord is the beginning of knowledge. — Proverbs 1:7.

The mother's heart is the child's schoolroom. — Henry Ward Beecher

The principle mark of genius is not perfection but originality, the opening of new frontiers. — Arthur Koestler

There is something fascinating about science. One gets such wholesale returns of conjecture out of such a trifling investment of fact. — Mark Twain

The smartest people know that God knows best. — *ODB*, July 2006.

Training is everything. The peach was once a bitter almond; cauliflower is nothing but cabbage with a college education. — Mark Twain

Truth is more of a stranger than fiction. — Mark Twain

When in doubt, tell the truth. — Mark Twain

When pride comes, then comes disgrace, but with humility comes wisdom. — Proverbs 11:2.

Wisdom is knowing when to speak your mind and when to mind your speech. — *ODB*, February 2003.

You can gain knowledge on your own, but wisdom comes from God. — *ODB*, June 2003.

Love

A big part of loving is listening. — *ODB*, March 2003.

A healthy heart beats with love for Jesus. — *ODB*, August 2005.

A little love can make a big difference. — *ODB*, June 2005.

At the touch of love, everyone becomes a poet. — Plato

Compassion is love in action. — *ODB*, September 2004.

Compassion is needed to heal the hurts and hearts of others. — *ODB*, July 2006.

God loves us too much to let us stay as we are. — *ODB*, April 2002.

I love you not only for what you are, but for what I am because of you. — Jo Petty, *Bits of Silver and Gold, Love.*

If you ask, "Is life worth living?" you have never loved. — Jo Petty, *Bits of Silver and Gold, Love.*

Listen to understand, then speak with love. — *ODB*, June 2003.

Love is:
- Caring what happens and doing something about it.
- reaching out
- encouraging the downhearted
- drawing near
- warm acceptance of another—as is
- contact—getting in touch

— Unknown

Love doesn't make the world go round. Love makes the ride worthwhile.
— Elizabeth Barrett Browning

Love helps people even when it hurts. — *ODB*, March 2005.

Love in return for love is natural, but love in return for hate is supernatural. — *ODB*, August 2005.

Love increases as we give it away. — *ODB*, February 2002.

Love is a conquering force. — Jo Petty, *Bits of Silver and Gold, Love.*

Love isn't divided when it's shared. It grows larger. — Unknown

Love is patient, love is kind. It does not envy, it does not boast, it is not proud. It is not rude, it is not self-seeking, it is not easily angered, it keeps not record of wrongs. — 1 Corinthians 13:4-5.

Love's concern is with the revival of the unfit rather than the survival of the fittest. — Jo Petty, *Bits of Silver and Gold, Love.*

No door is too difficult for the key of love to open. — Jo Petty, *Bits of Silver and Gold, Love.*

Our identity is hidden in love, in a love that cannot exist at all until it gives itself away. — Unknown

Prejudice builds walls; love breaks them down. — *ODB*, May 2003.

Real love puts action to good intentions. — *ODB*, September 2005.

The best way to conquer an enemy is with the weapon of love. — *ODB*, June 2006.

The truth may hurt, but love helps ease the pain. — *ODB*, February 2003.

The worst kind of heart trouble is not to have love in your heart. — Jo Petty, *Bits of Silver and Gold, Love.*

There is a big difference between love and infatuation. — Unknown

They are the true disciples of Christ, not who know most, but who love most. — Frederich Spanheim

They do not truly love who do not show their love. — Shakespeare

To make a big difference in life, show a little love. — *ODB*, April 2002.

Truth spoken in love is hard to refuse. — *ODB*, February 2003.

When love flows, acceptance grows. — Chuck Swindoll, *Growing Strong in the Seasons of Life*, p. 415.

Marriage

A happy marriage is a union of two good forgivers. — *ODB*, October 2005.

A marriage is not a joining of two worlds, but an abandoning of two worlds in order that one new one might be formed. — Mike Mason, *The Mystery of Marriage*.

A successful marriage is an edifice that must be rebuilt every day. — André Maurois

A successful marriage requires falling in love many times, always with the same person. — *ODB*, December 2003; Mignon McLaughlin; Jo Petty, *Bits of Silver and Gold, Love.*

Any man who thinks he is more intelligent than his wife is married to a smart woman. — Jo Petty, *Bits of Silver and Gold, Love.*

Happiness is being married to your best friend. — Barbara Weeks

Jesus Christ is the only third party in a marriage who can make it work. — *ODB*, August 2006.

Love and commitment deepen as two people work toward common goals in a marriage. — Chuck Swindoll, *Stress Fractures*, p. 145.

Love is blind, but marriage is a real eye-opener. — Paula Deen

Marriage does not affect people like people affect marriage. — Jo Petty, *Bits of Silver and Gold, Love.*

Marriage is built with special kind of bricks, bricks of communication, love, patience, understanding, and above all the brick of forgiveness. — Unknown

Marriages may be made in heaven, but they have to be worked out on earth. — *ODB*, February 2003.

Matrimony is the high sea for which no compass has been invented. — Jo Petty, *Bits of Silver and Gold, Love.*

Nurture your marriage and you'll nourish your soul. — *ODB*, September 2005.

Success in marriage is not finding the right person but becoming the right person. — *ODB*, May 2003.

Surrendering is not an option if you plan to win a war—or succeed in a marriage. — Chuck Swindoll, *Strike the Original Match*, p. 31.

There is no marital problem so great that God cannot solve it. — Chuck Swindoll, *Strike the Original Match*, p. 135.

To keep harmony in your marriage, keep in tune with Christ. — *ODB*, February 2002.

Money and Possessions ("Stuff")

All we own is on loan from God. — *ODB*, December 2004.

Contentment comes not from great wealth but from few wants. — *ODB*, March 2001, January 2003.

Do we love things and use people or love people and use things? — Jo Petty, *Bits of Silver and Gold, Love.*

Everything you own means that much more trouble for you. — Unknown

For a quick check on your heart, check out your checkbook. — *ODB*, May 2005.

Hold everything earthly with a loose hand. — C. H. Spurgeon

I do not believe one can settle how much we ought to give. I am afraid the only safe rule is to give more than we can spare. — C. S. Lewis

If you want to be rich, count all the things you have that money can't buy. — *ODB*, July 2005.

Life is more than the things we store. — *ODB*, November 2003.

Money can't buy you happiness, but it does bring you a more pleasant form of misery. — Mortimer B. Zuckerman, "Words to Live By," *U.S. News & World Report*, January 2006.

Money is a good servant but a bad master. — French Proverb

The amount of a man's wealth consists of the number of things he can do without. — Unkown

The best thing to spend on children is time. — Jo Petty, *Bits of Silver and Gold, Love.*

The best way to live happily ever after is not to be after too much. — Unknown

The true measure of our wealth is the treasure we have in heaven. — *ODB*, January 2003, July 2004.

Those who lay up treasures in heaven are the richest people on earth. — *ODB*, June 2005.

True contentment is not in having everything, but in being satisfied with everything you have. — *ODB*, May 2003.

Wealth is a double blessing when it's used for the blessing of others. — *ODB*, February 2002.

You can't store up treasures in heaven if you're holding on to the treasures of earth. — *ODB*, February 2003.

Your standard of giving is more important than your standard of living. — *ODB*, February 2005.

Parenting

A child is likely to see God as a good father if he sees God in his father.
— *ODB*, June 2002.

A Christlike example is the greatest gift parents can give their children.
— *ODB*, June 2000, May 2001.

A life lived for Christ is the best inheritance we can leave our children.
— *ODB*, June 2002.

Always be nice to your children because they are the ones that will choose your rest home. — Phyllis Diller

A mother's primary goal should be to work herself out of a job. — Unknown

Believe in them—they'll believe in themselves. — Unknown

Character traits are sculptured under the watchful eyes of moms and dads.

Determination	Stick with it, regardless.
Honesty	Speak and live the truth—always.
Responsibility	Be dependable, be trustworthy.
Thoughtfulness	Think of others before yourself.
Confidentiality	Don't tell secrets.
Punctuality	Be on time.
Self-control	When under stress, stay calm.
Patience	Fight irritability. Be willing to wait.
Purity	Reject anything that lowers your standards.
Compassion	When another hurts, feel it with him.
Diligence	Work hard. Tough it out.

— Chuck Swindoll, *Growing Strong in the Seasons of Life*, p. 392.

Children are more likely to do what you do than to do what you say. — *ODB*, October 2001.

Children's ears may be closed to advice, but their eyes are open to example. — *ODB*, October 2002.

Encourage responsibility. — Unknown

Fathers, do not exasperate your children; instead, bring them up in the training and instruction of the Lord. — Ephesians 6:4.

Find out where their strength is, what they have a bent for. Then you take away whatever interferes with that bent so it can develop naturally. — Unknown

Give your kids all the sunshine, and give Jesus all the rest. — Unknown

Good fathers make good sons. — Jacob M. Braude

Good fathers not only tell us how to live—they show us. — *ODB*, June 2002.

If you can give your son or daughter only one gift, let it be enthusiasm. — Bruce Barton

If you haven't time to help youngsters find the right way in life, somebody with more time will help them find the wrong way. — Frank A. Clark

If you want to see what your children can do, you must stop giving them things. — Norman Douglas

I take my children everywhere, but they always find their way back home. — Robert Orben

It is not giving children more that spoils them; it is giving them more to avoid confrontation. — John Gray

It's tough when children stomp on your heart. Hope in your heart will keep you alive. — Mark 11:23–24.

Lessons learned at a mother's knee last through life. — Laura Ingalls Wilder

Level with your child by being honest. Nobody spots a phony quicker than a child. — Mary MacCracken

Life affords no greater responsibility, no greater privilege, than the raising of the next generation. — C. Everett Koop

Yelling at your kids to get them to obey makes as much sense as driving your car by honking the horn. — Unknown

Motherhood is a sacred partnership with God. — *ODB*, May 2003.

On children: The less you fuss over things they're going to outgrow anyway, the better. If you fuss too much, you watch, they'll do it again just for excitement. — Unknown

On training up teenagers—lock them in a closet with a copy of Proverbs.

One mother achieves more than a hundred teachers. — Yiddish Proverb

Parenting—It might be best to consult the "manufacturer" when it comes to seeking advice on the "product." God is the creator of children (Psalm 139:14–16) and has filled the Bible with precepts and examples on how to guide them to maturity—maturity meaning adults who choose to love God through His Son, Jesus Christ. — David Jeremiah

Parents should work together as efficiently as two bookends. — Jacob M. Braude

Parents who are always giving their children nothing but the best usually wind up with nothing but the worst. — Jacob M. Braude

Show me your friends, and I will show you your future. — John Kuebler, Pastor, Trinity Presbyterian Church, Charlottesville, VA

Spare the rod and spoil the child—that is true. But, beside the rod, keep an apple to give him when he has done well. — Martin Luther

Spoiled children are given what they want; wise parents give them what they need. — *ODB*, March 2003.

The best fathers not only give us life—they teach us how to live. — *ODB*, June 2005.

The best safeguard for the younger generation is a good example by the older generation. — *ODB*, September 2003.

The best thing you spend on your children is your time. — *ODB*, July 2004; Jo Petty, *Bits of Silver and Gold, Love.*

The character of your children tomorrow depends on what you put into their hearts today. — *ODB*, July 2003.

The greatest gifts you can give your children are the roots of responsibility and the wings of independence. — Denis Waitley

The mother is and must be, whether she knows it or not, the greatest, strongest, and most lasting teacher her children can have. — Laura Ingalls Wilder

There are only two lasting bequests we give our children; one is roots, the other, wings. — Hodding Carter

The reason grandparents and grandchildren get along so well is that they have a common enemy. — Sam Levenson

The responsible parent knows that all the love in the world will not compensate the child who has not learned to fear the consequences of his own behavior. It takes some abrasive to polish a gem. — Jo Petty, *Bits of Silver and Gold, Love.*

There was a time when we expected nothing of our children but obedience, as opposed to the present, when we expect everything of them but obedience. — Anatole Broyard

The richest inheritance a grandparent can leave is a godly example. — *ODB*, September 2003.

The secret of good parenting is consistency. Never forget that! Stay at it, day in and day out. — Chuck Swindoll, *Growing Strong in the Seasons of Life*, p. 394.

The surest way to make life hard for your children is to make it soft for them. — *ODB*, June 2001.

The thing that impresses me the most about America is the way parents obey their children. — King Edward VIII

The values we leave in our children are more important than the valuables we leave to them. — *ODB*, September 2001.

Too many parents are not on spanking terms with their children. — Jacob M. Braude

Train a child in the way he is, according to his own nature and distinctiveness. — Unknown

Train a child in the way he should go, and when he is old he will not turn from it. — Proverbs 22:6.

Train up a child in the way he should go, but be sure you go that way yourself. — *ODB*, September 2000, November 2006.

Treat a child as though he already is the person he's capable of becoming. — Haim Ginott

We are to guide our children to transfer their sense of responsibility and accountability from the parent to Almighty God. — Unknown

We can't share with our children what we don't know ourselves. — Unknown

We love our children, but are we teaching them to be loving? — Jo Petty, *Bits of Silver and Gold, Love.*

We shape tomorrow's world by what we teach our children today. — *ODB*, January 2002.

What we leave in our children is more important than what we leave to them. — *ODB*, October 2003.

You can't protect them from the elements, but you can understand what they're up against and guide them so they will bend and not break. — Unknown

Your biggest investment may be helping a little child. — *ODB*, October 2000.

Prayer

A day hemmed in prayer is less likely to unravel. — John and Denny, Family Life Network

Any concern too small to be turned into a prayer is too small to be made into a burden. — Corrie ten Boom

A Sunday school teacher asked her young class, "What is prayer?" One of her pupils answered, "That's a message sent to God at night and on Sundays, when the rates are lower." — Paul Heil

Every child needs a praying parent. — *ODB*, November 2003.

God's answers are often wiser than our prayers. — *ODB*, April 2002.

I have been driven many times to my knees, by the overwhelming conviction that I had nowhere else to go. My own wisdom, and that of all about me seemed insufficient for that day. — Abraham Lincoln

In the face of danger, face danger with prayer. — *ODB*, May 2002.

I remember my mother's prayers … They have clung to me all my life. — Abraham Lincoln

Is prayer your steering wheel or your spare tire? — Corrie ten Boom

It's not the words we pray that matter, it's the condition of our heart. — *ODB*, June 2005.

Keep us, God, for your ocean is wide, and our boat is small. — Sailor's Prayer

Life's best outlook is a prayerful uplook. — *ODB*, January 2003.

Never pray for money. The Lord is your shepherd, not your banker. — Unknown

Pray as you can, not as you can't. — Dom Chapman

Prayer isn't a time to give orders but to report for duty. — *ODB*, March 2005.

Prayer should be our first response rather than our last resort. — *ODB*, December 2003.

Religion is no more possible without prayer than poetry without language, or music without atmosphere. — James Martineau

Seven days without prayer makes one weak. — Allen E. Vartlett

The purpose of prayer is not to get what we want, but to become what God wants. — *ODB*, January 2003.

There is no more significant involvement in another's life than prevailing, consistent prayer. — Chuck Swindoll, *The Quest for Character*, p. 132.

When life knocks you to your knees, you're in a good position to pray. — *ODB*, May 2004.

When you pray, don't give God orders—report for duty. — Unknown

Work as if you'll live to be a hundred. Pray as if you'll die tomorrow. — Benjamin Franklin

Salvation

. . . for all have sinned and fall short of the glory of God, and are justified freely by His grace through the redemption that came by Jesus Christ. — Romans 3:23-24.

Believing Christ died—that's history; believing He died for me—that's salvation. — *ODB*, November 2004.

Calvary's cross is the only bridge to eternal life. — *ODB*, January 2002.

Don't plan to repent at the eleventh hour—you may die at 10:30. — *ODB*, October 2002.

Everyone who calls on the name of the Lord will be saved. — Joel 2:32.

For the Christian, death is the doorway to glory. — *ODB*, February 2003.

Give your life to Christ and you'll keep it forever. — *ODB*, September 2006.

God's people never say good-bye for the last time. — *ODB*, September 2005.

He is no fool who gives what he cannot keep to gain what he cannot lose. — Jim Elliot

In a world of smoke and mirrors, Jesus offers the miracle of salvation. — *ODB*, September 2005.

Is death the last sleep? No, it is the last final awakening. — Sir Walter Scott

Is there any hope for lost sinners? Yes, Christ. Not Christ and the church. Not Christ and good works. Not Christ and sincerity. Not Christ and giving up your sins. Not Christ and trying real hard. Not Christ and baptism, Christ and christening, Christ and morality, or Christ and a good family. No! Christ period! — Chuck Swindoll, *Growing Deep in the Christian Life*, p. 243.

It is better to limp all the way to heaven than to not get there at all. — Billy Sunday

It's not enough to know the facts of salvation—you must know the Savior. — *ODB*, February 2003.

Jesus answered, "I am the way and the truth and the life. No one comes to the Father except through me." — John 14:6.

Jesus took our place on the cross to give us a place in heaven. — *ODB*, February 2003.

Life's biggest decision is what you do with Jesus. — *ODB*, June 2006.

No one is good enough to save himself; no one is so bad that God cannot save him. — *ODB*, January 2003.

One thought comforts us—where they have gone, we are going forever. — Unknown

Salvation is a gift that anyone can open. — *ODB*, September 2004.

Salvation is simply a gift. It's simple, but it wasn't easy. It's free, but it wasn't cheap. It's yours, but it isn't automatic. You must receive it.

Lois E. Scott

When you do, it is yours forever. — Chuck Swindoll, *Growing Deep in the Christian Life*, p. 244.

Satan scrambles the signals of salvation. — Unknown

Thanks be to God for His indescribable gift! — 2 Corinthians 9:15.

The pathway to heaven begins at the foot of the cross. — *ODB*, March 2002.

We all need salvation, whether we're nice or not. — *ODB*, September 2003.

We are saved by God's mercy, not by our merit—by Christ's dying, not by our doing. — *ODB*, May 2003.

We believe it is through the grace of our Lord Jesus that we are saved. — Acts 15:11.

We can really live if we are ready to die. — *ODB*, September 2005.

When Jesus comes into a life, He changes everything. — *ODB*, March 2002.

You can have tons of religion without an ounce of salvation. — *ODB*, June 2001, July 2003.

Sin and Temptation

Forbidden fruit tastes sweet, but its aftertaste is bitter. — *ODB*, July 2003.

God's Spirit is your power source—don't let sin break the connection. — *ODB*, September 2006.

If you yield to God, you won't give in to sin. — *ODB*, June 2005.

In spite of inflation, the wages of sin have not changed. — Unknown

Little sins won't stay little. — *ODB*, August 2003.

Lois E. Scott

Most of us are far-sighted about sin—we see the sins of others but not our own. — *ODB*, January 2004.

Most often, falling into sin is not a blowout but a slow leak. — *ODB*, June 2001.

One bite of sin leaves a bitter aftertaste. — *ODB*, September 2005.

One sin rationalized becomes two. — *ODB*, November 2004.

Our greatest freedom is freedom from sin. — *ODB*, July 2003.

Repentance means hating sin enough to turn from it. — *ODB*, September 2005.

Run! It is impossible to yield to temptation while running in the opposite direction. — Chuck Swindoll, *Stress Fractures*, p. 124.

Sin adds to your troubles, subtracts from your energy, and multiplies your difficulties. — *ODB*, March 2002.

Sins are kinda like rabbits—turn a couple of 'em loose and the first thing you know there's a whole bunch of new ones. — Frank A. Clark

There's no excuse for excusing sin. — *ODB*, September 2003.

To master temptation, keep your eyes on the Master. — *ODB*, July 2003.

When we sow seeds of sin, we can count on a harvest of judgment. — *ODB*, September 2005.

When you flee temptation, be sure you don't leave a forwarding address. — *ODB*, April 2001.

Thanksgiving

Enter His gates with thanksgiving and His courts with praise; give thanks to Him and praise His name. — Psalm 100:4.

Give thanks to the Lord, for He is good; His love endures forever. — Psalm 107:1.

Instead of grumbling because you don't get what you want, be thankful you don't get what you deserve. — *ODB*, March 2004.

Joy is a fruit of the Spirit that's always in season. — *ODB*, March 2006.

Let us come before Him with thanksgiving and extol Him with music and song. — Psalm 95:2.

Thankfulness begins with a good memory. — *ODB*, July 2003.

Work

All anybody needs to know about prizes is that Mozart never won one. — Henry Mitchell

All Christians have the same employer—they just have different jobs. — *ODB*, June 2003.

Don't waste time learning the "tricks of the trade." Instead, learn the trade. — H. Jackson Brown, Jr.

For the Christian, work is ministry. — *ODB*, June 2006.

God is looking for ordinary people to do extraordinary work. — *ODB*, June 2005.

Humble work becomes holy work when it's done for God. — *ODB*, March 2001.

If you don't have time to do it right, when will you have time to do it over? — John Woodon

If you shirk today's tasks, you increase tomorrow's burdens. — *ODB*, June 2003.

It is not the hours you put in that count, but what you put in the hours. — *ODB*, February 2003, September 2005.

Just as there are no little people or unimportant lives, there is no insignificant work. — Elena Bonner

No matter who your boss is, you are really working for God. — *ODB*, September 2001.

No one else can do the work God has for you. — *ODB*, May 2002.

Nothing is work unless you'd rather be doing something else. — George Halas

Pray as if everything depends on God; work as if everything depends on you. — *ODB*, May 2005.

Some people stop looking for work when they get a job. — *ODB*, July 2003.

Success is going from failure to failure without loss of enthusiasm. — Winston Churchill

The best cure for insomnia is a Monday morning. — Sandy Cooley

The future belongs to those who are willing to work for it. — Unknown

The highest reward for a person's toil is not what they get for it, but what they become by it. — John Ruskin

The world crowns success; God crowns faithfulness. — *ODB*, June 2003.

There is not an achievement worth remembering that isn't stained with the blood of diligence and etched with the scars of disappointment. — Chuck Swindoll, *Come Before Winter*, p. 181.

To work in the ice cream parlor you have to attend sundae school. — Larry Laukhuf

Lois E. Scott

When people are more important than profits, everyone profits. — *ODB*, September 2003.

When there is work to be done, turn up your sleeves, not your nose. — Unknown

Work done well will receive God's "Well done." — *ODB*, November 2005.

Work is a blessing when it blesses others. — *ODB*, June 2005.

Worship

Come, let us bow down in worship, let us kneel before the Lord our Maker; for He is our God and we are the people of His pasture, and the flock under His care. — Psalm 95:6-7.

There are many ways to worship God, but only one God to worship. — *ODB*, January 2004.

We have become a generation of people who worship our work, who work at our play, and who play at our worship. — Chuck Swindoll, *Stress Fractures,* p. 157.

What you worship determines what you become. — *ODB*, January 2001.

Worship on Sunday morning should begin on Saturday night. — *ODB*, January 2003.

Selected Sources

Campus Crusade for Christ International. <www.ccci.org/wij/index.aspx>.

Miller, Robert M. *The Best of RMM: Vol.1–The Doctor Will Be Right Out; Vol. 2–V.W.H.S.T.C.* American Veterinary Publications, Wheaton, IL, 1960.

Our Daily Bread. RBC Ministries, P.O. Box 2222, Grand Rapids, MI 49501-2222, <www.rbc.net>.

Petty, Jo. *Bits of Silver and Gold; Love.* The C.R. Gibson Co., Norwalk, CT.

Swindoll, Charles R. *Come Before Winter and Share My Hope.* Zondervan Publishing, Grand Rapids, MI, <www.zondervan.com>.

Swindoll, Charles R. *Encourage Me.* Zondervan Publishing, Grand Rapids, MI, <www.zondervan.com>.

Swindoll, Charles R. *Growing Deep in the Christian Life.* Zondervan Publishing, Grand Rapids, MI, <www.zondervan.com>.

Swindoll, Charles R. *Growing Strong in the Seasons of Life.* Zondervan Publishing, Grand Rapids, MI, <www.zondervan.com>.

Swindoll, Charles R. *Growing Wise in Family Life.* Zondervan Publishing, Grand Rapids, MI, <www.zondervan.com>.

Swindoll, Charles R. *Home: Where Life Makes Up Its Mind*. Zondervan Publishing, Grand Rapids, MI, <www.zondervan.com>.

Swindoll, Charles R. *Rise and Shine*. Zondervan Publishing, Grand Rapids, MI, <www.zondervan.com>.

Swindoll, Charles R. *Stress Fractures*. Zondervan Publishing, Grand Rapids, MI, <www.zondervan.com>.

Swindoll, Charles R. *Strike the Original Match*. Zondervan Publishing, Grand Rapids, MI, <www.zondervan.com>.

Swindoll, Charles R. *The Quest for Character*. Zondervan Publishing, Grand Rapids, MI, <www.zondervan.com>.

The Holy Bible: New International Version. Zondervan Bible Publishers, Grand Rapids, MI, 1978.

Warren, Rick. *The Purpose Driven Church*. Zondervan Publishing, Grand Rapids, MI, 1995.

Conclusion

Without a heritage, every generation starts over. Generations come and generations go. Each person is dealt a portion, or a hand to play, some good, some difficult. Each person acquires a certain degree of success and wealth, and then death eventually and inevitably comes to all. Each person leaves a legacy, good or bad, to those who come behind. This legacy may include name and reputation, children and grandchildren, wealth and worldly possessions, and faith and faithfulness. Investment in the lives of others is the only thing that lasts forever.

The words of a hymn by Jon Mohr are apropos for our relationship with our children and friends.

Find Us Faithful
Hymn by Jon Mohr
O may all who come behind us find us faithful;
May the fire of our devotion light their way.
May the footprints that we leave lead them to believe,
And the lives we live inspire them to obey.
O may all who come behind us find us faithful.

We hope these gems have given the reader a laugh or two and provided some food for thought as you live your life and raise your children. If you have not yet come to a saving relationship with the living Christ, we urge you to contemplate your relationship with Him, and hence your future beyond this limited time you have on this Earth.

Printed in the United States
By Bookmasters